Hamilton Ontario Book 2 in Colour Photos, Saving Our History One Photo at a Time

Photography
by Barbara Raué
updated 2016

Series Name:
Cruising Ontario

Book 88: Hamilton Book 2

Cover photo: 30-32 Erie Avenue, Page 38

Series Name: Cruising Ontario
Saving Our History One Photo at a Time
in colour photos

Book 33: Southampton

Book 34: Jarvis

Book 35: Hagersville

Book 36: Caledonia

Book 37: Simcoe

Book 38-41: Cambridge

Book 42-43: Kitchener

Book 46: Shelburne

Book 47: Alton, Mono

Book 48: London Colour

Book 49: St. Thomas

Book 50-52: Orangeville

Book 53-55: Dundas

Book 56: Stratford

Book 57: Hanover

Book 58-59: New Hamburg

Book 60: Waterdown

Book 61: Burlington

Book 62: Stoney Creek

Book 63: Seaforth

Book 64: Aberfoyle, Morriston and Rockton

Book 65: Eden Mills

Book 66: Ancaster and Mount Hope

Book 67: Jarvis,Pt.Dover

Book 68-69: Fergus, Elora

Book 70-71: Elmira

Book72:St.Jacobs, St.Clements, Heidelberg,Crosshill,Bamberg

Book 73: Linwood, Macton

Book 74: Wellesley

Book 75: Listowel

Book 76: Palmerston

Book 77:Dorchester to Aylmer

Book 78-79: Aylmer

Book 80: Drayton & Area

Book 81: Tillsonburg

Book 82: Arthur

Book 83: Rockwood

Book 84: Acton

Book 85-86: Guelph

Book 87-91: Hamilton

Other Books by Barbara Raue

Coins of Gold

Arrows, Indians and Love

The Life and Times of Barbara
Volume 1: Inventions That Have Enhanced My Life
Volume 2: Entertainment That I Have Enjoyed
Volume 3: East Coast Trips
Volume 4: Olympics Have Always Intrigued Me
Volume 5: Wonders of the World
Volume 6: Caribbean Cruises We Have Enjoyed
Volume 7: Animals
Volume 8: Storms and Other Major Disasters in My Lifetime
Volume 9: Wars, Terrorist Attacks and Major Disasters

The Cromwell Family Book

Laura Secord Discovered

Daddy Where Are You?

Montana Series
Book 1: Montana Dream
Book 2: Life on the Montana Frontier
Book 3: Montana to Boston and Back

Visit Barbara's website to view all of her books
http://barbararaue.ca

Hamilton, the center of a densely populated and industrialized region, is located in Southern Ontario on the western part of Lake Ontario. Hamilton Harbor marks the northern limit of the city, and the Niagara Escarpment runs through the middle of the city bisecting the city into "upper" and "lower" parts. There are over one hundred waterfalls and cascades within the city, most of which are on or near the Bruce Trail as it winds through the Niagara Escarpment.

Two steel manufacturing companies, Stelco and Dofasco, were formed in 1910 and 1912, and Procter & Gamble opened a manufacturing plant in 1914. McMaster University moved from Toronto to Hamilton, an airport was built in 1940, a Studebaker assembly line started in 1948, the Burlington Bay Skyway Bridge was built in 1958, and the first Tim Horton's store opened in 1964.

The city experienced a devastating fire at the Plastimet plastics plant in 1997 with about three hundred firefighters battling the blaze on Wellington Street North when tons of PVC Plastic caught on fire.

On January 1, 2001, the new City of Hamilton was formed through the amalgamation of the former city and the six municipalities of Stoney Creek, Glanbrook which includes Mount Hope, Ancaster, Dundas, and Flamborough which includes Waterdown.

Hamilton is home to the Royal Botanical Gardens, McMaster University and Mohawk College. The Canadian Football League's Hamilton Tiger Cats began playing at the new Tim Hortons Field in 2014, which was built as part of the 2015 Pan American Games which will be jointly hosted by Toronto and Hamilton. We have lived in Hamilton for more than 40 years; it is here that we raised our three children.

Table of Contents

McMaster University – incorporated in 1887

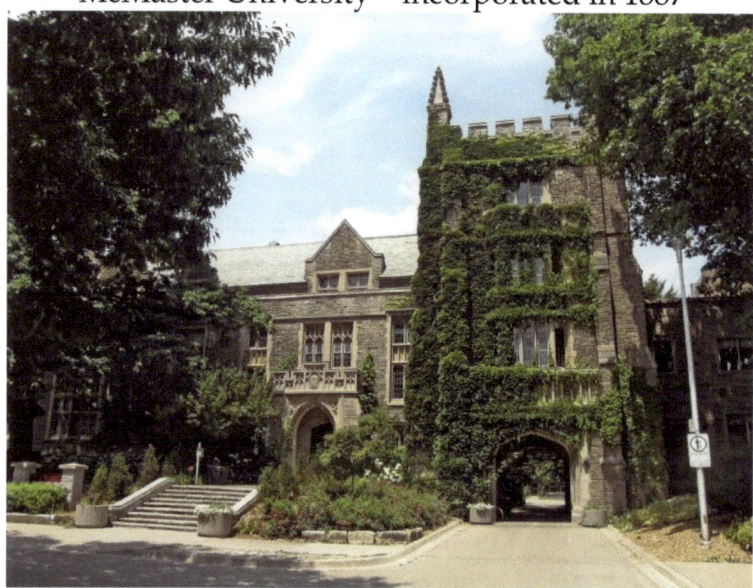

University Hall – Neo-Gothic or Collegiate Gothic style - tower is supported by large buttresses; parapet has battlementing and oversized finials; bay window has tracery, ogee curves, and a many muntins; the archway has a beautifully carved reveal and spandrels that contain images to inspire learning

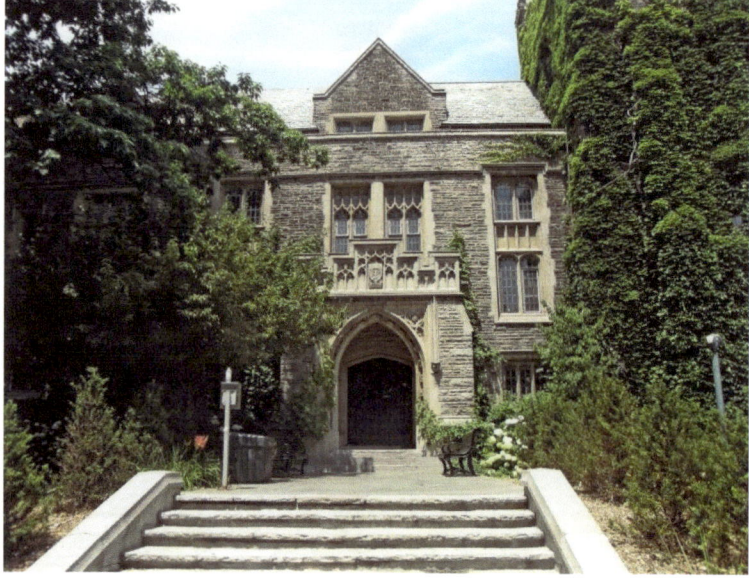

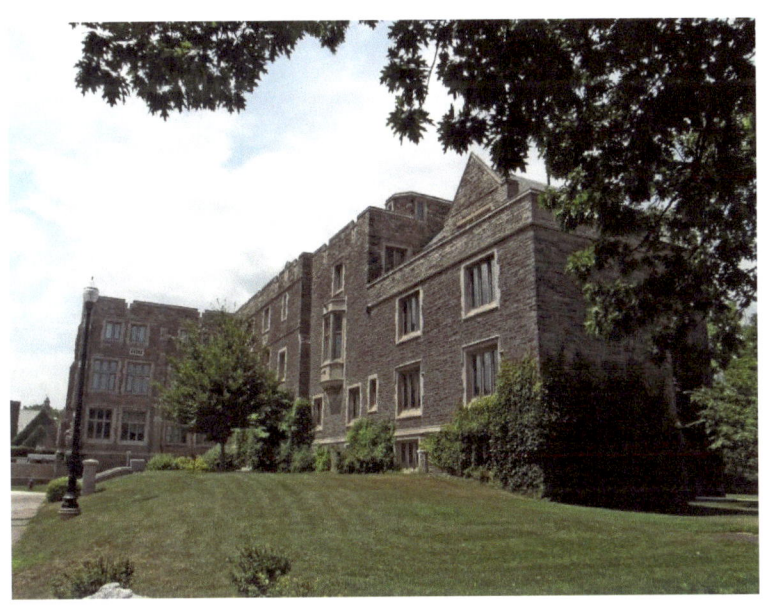

Hamilton Hall – Neo-Gothic or Collegiate Gothic style

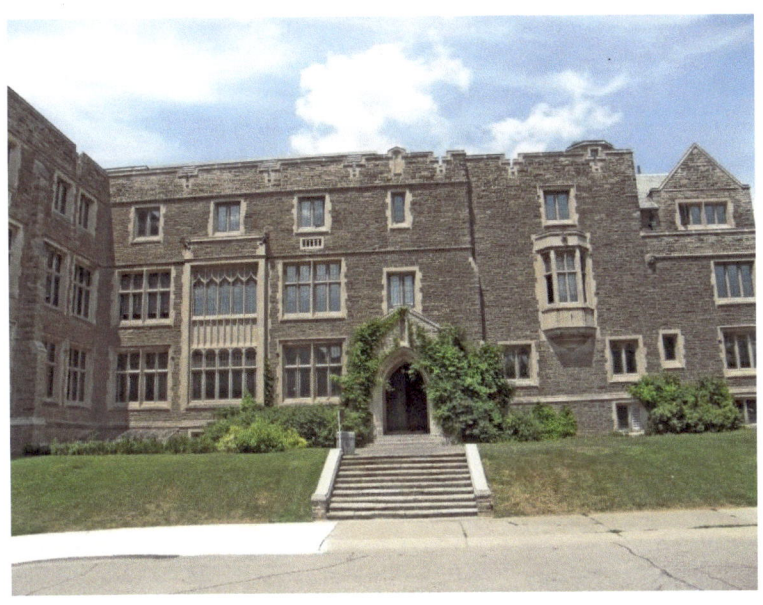

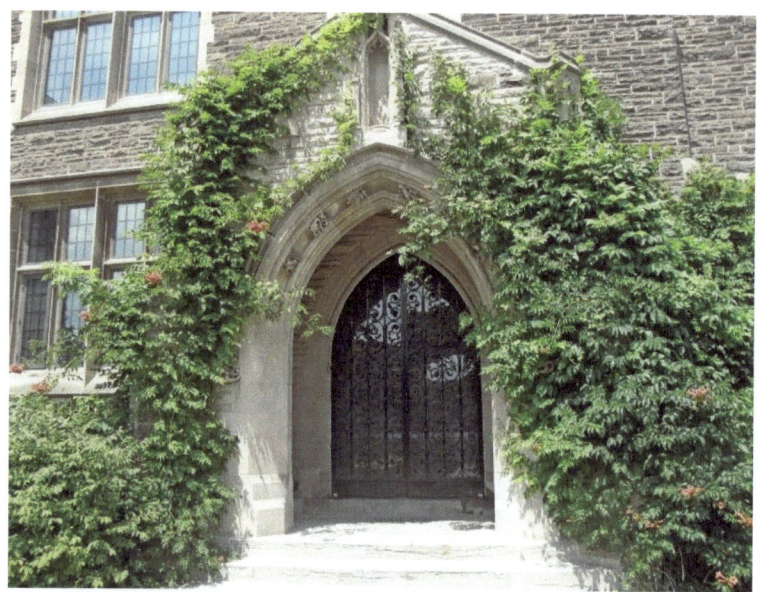

Hamilton Hall - the reveal has many carved moldings that represent the various disciplines studied at the university: the fish represent Biology, the pick ax and shovel for Mining Engineering, the wheelbarrow for Geology, etc. Neo-Gothic architecture lends itself well to education because of these detailing possibilities.

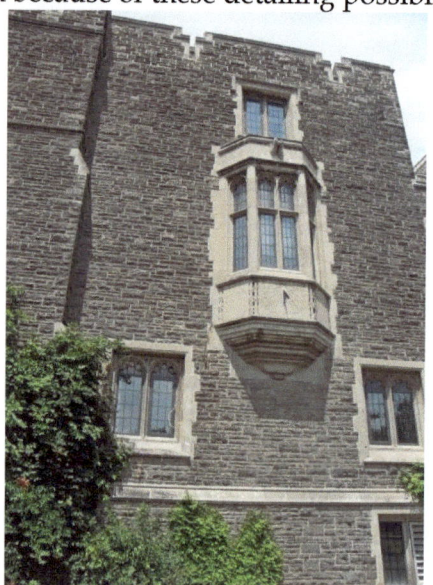

Oriel window

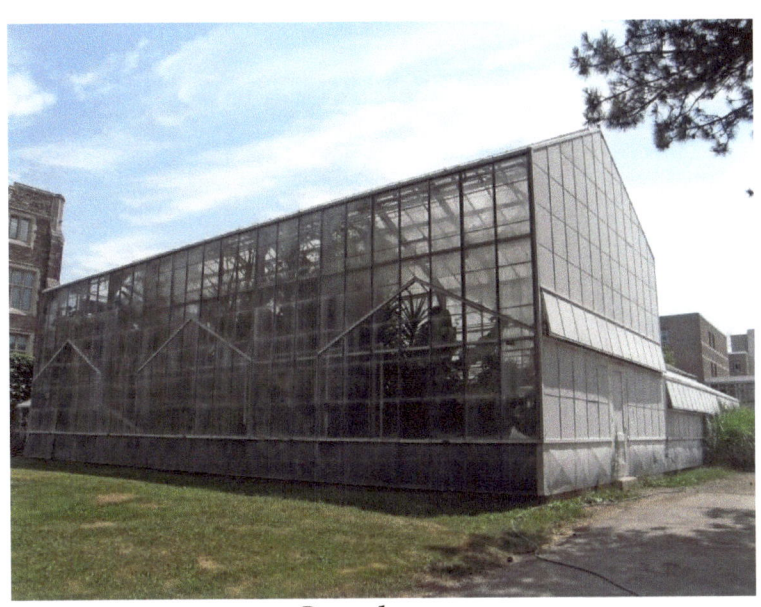

Greenhouses

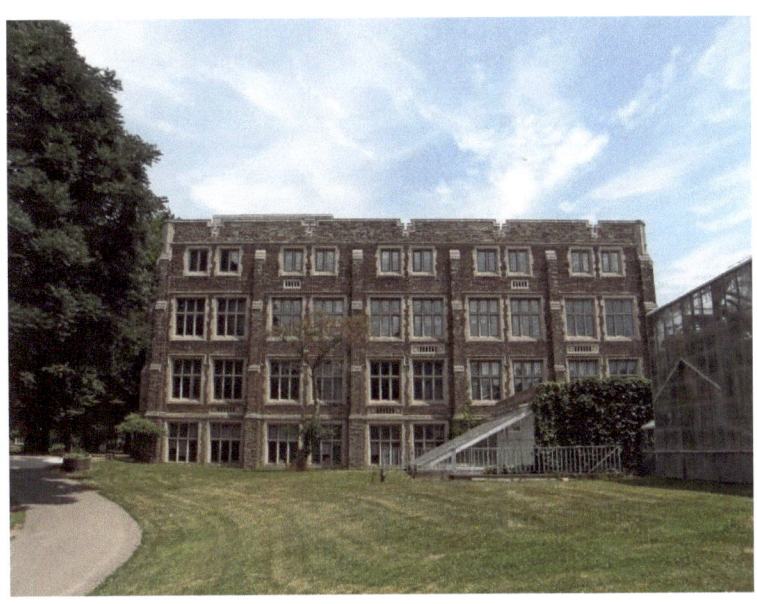

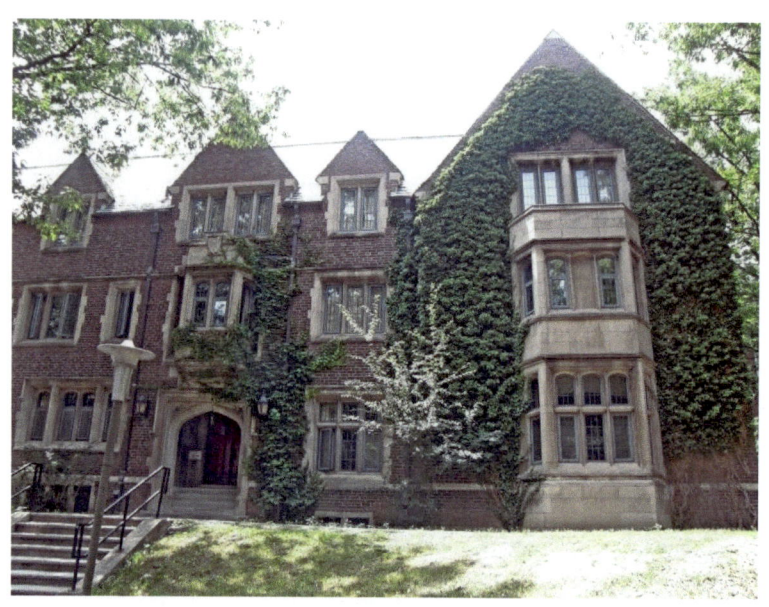

Old Residences - dormers

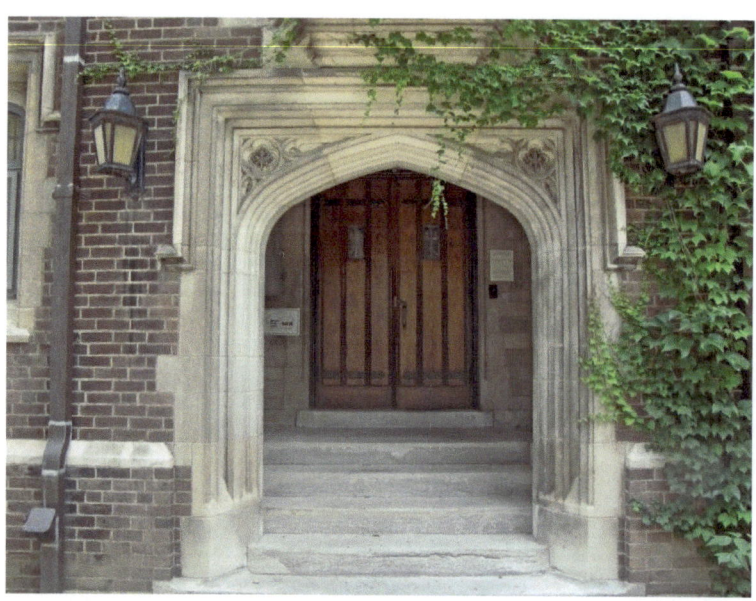

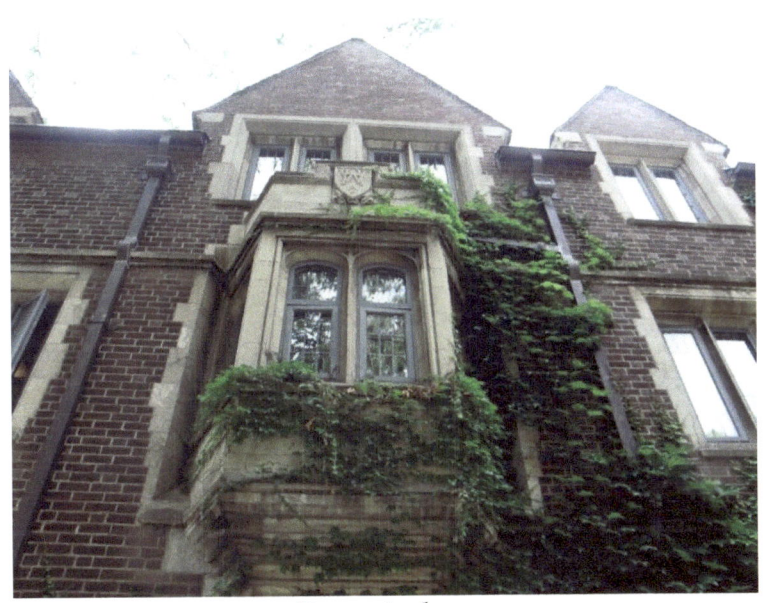

Bay window

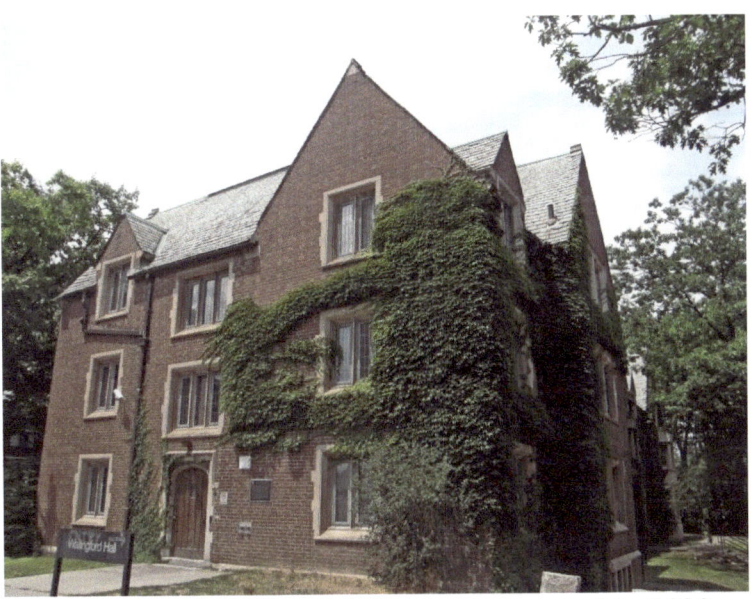

Wallingford Hall residence – constructed in 1930

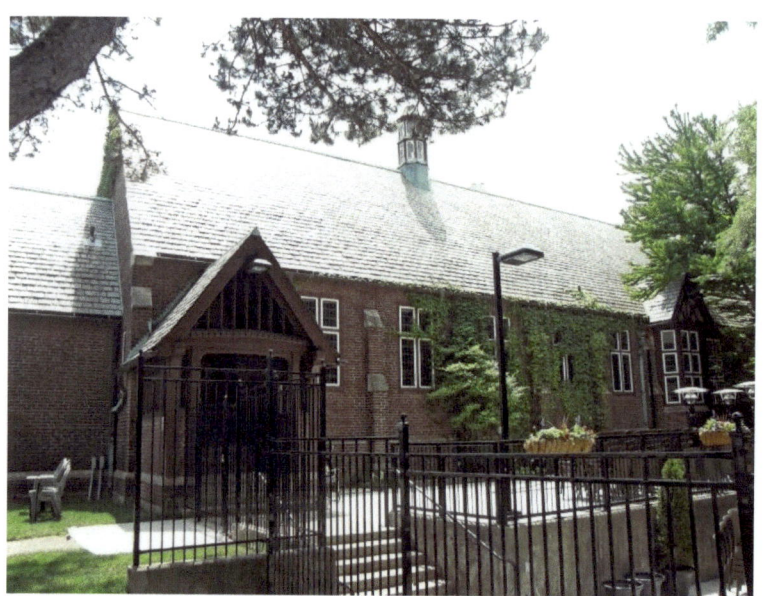

Refectory Rathskeller

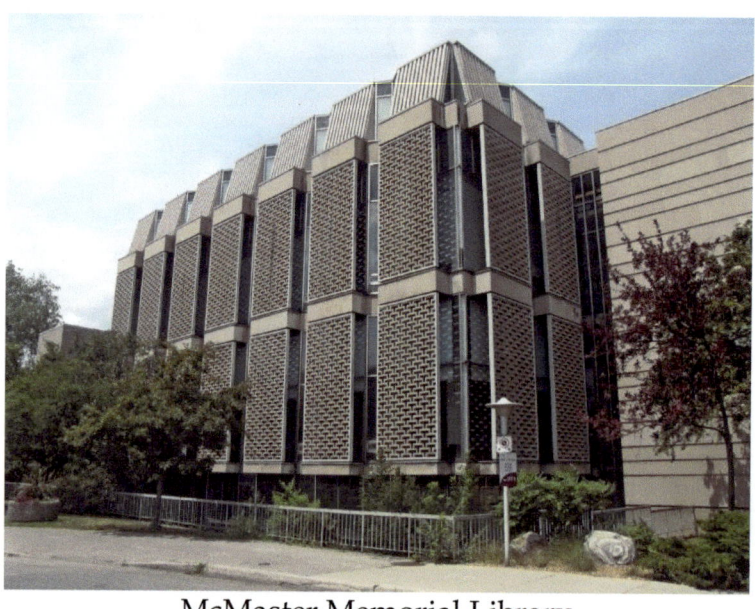

McMaster Memorial Library

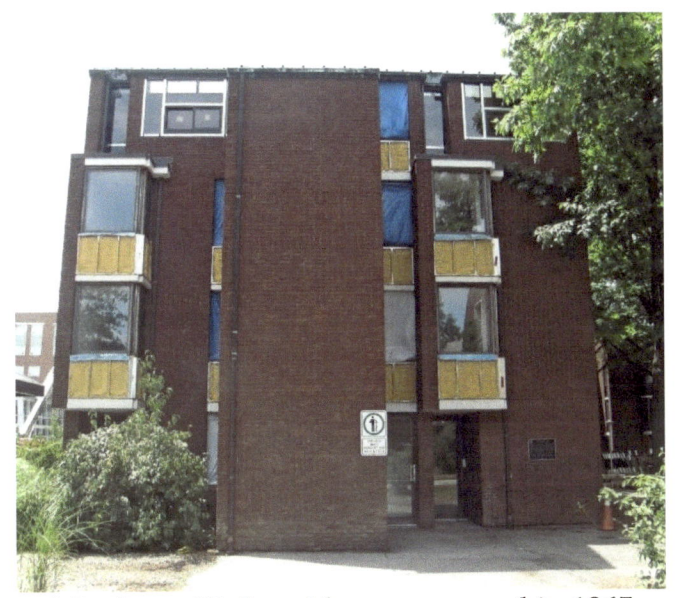

Matthews Hall residence – opened in 1965

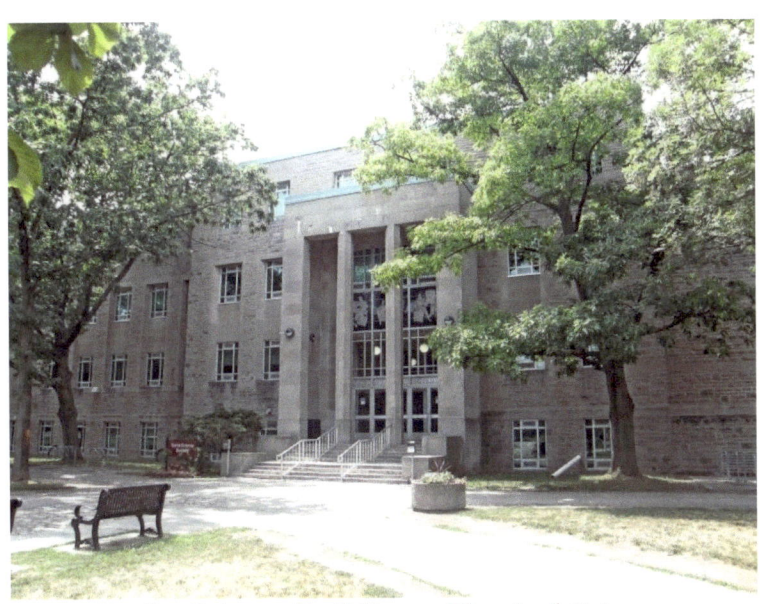

Burke Science Building – Physical Science

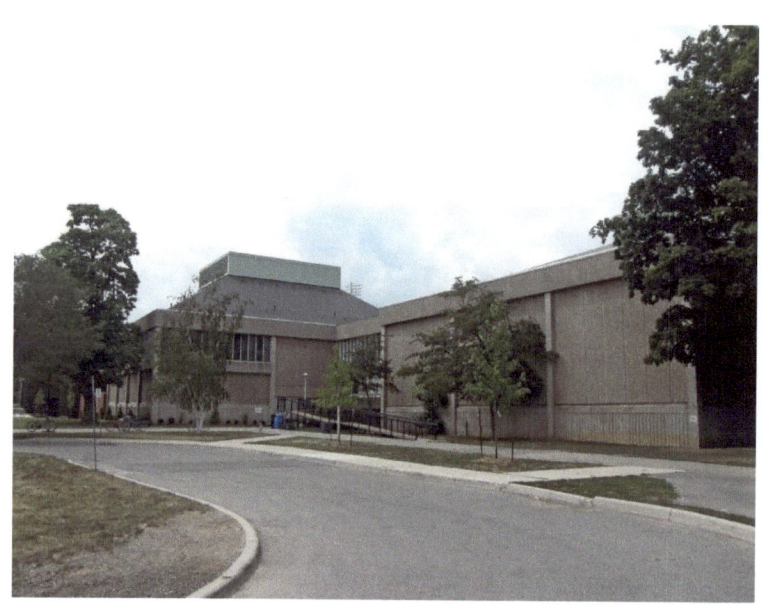

Swimming Pool

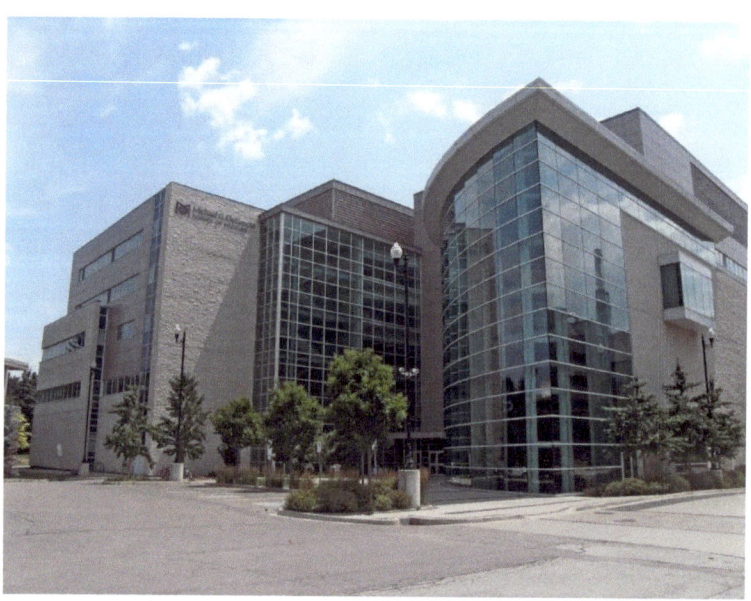

Michael G. DeGroote School of Medicine

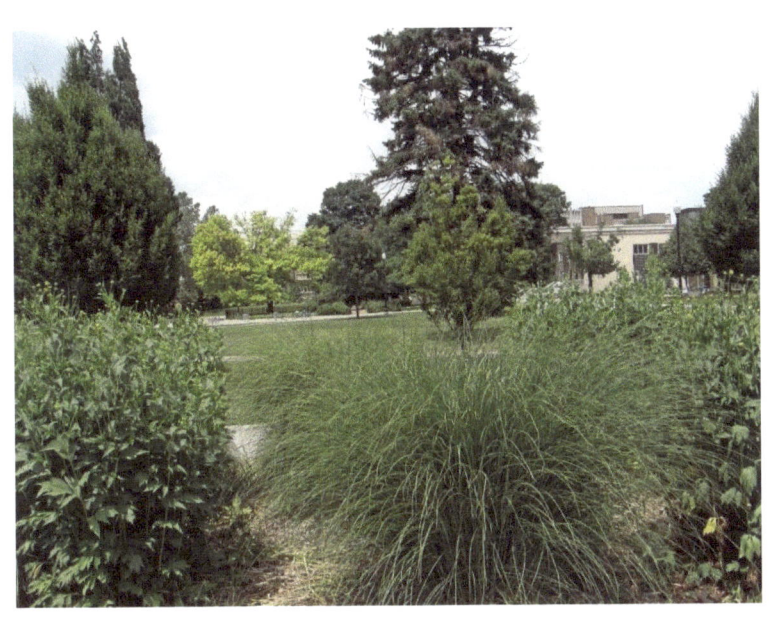

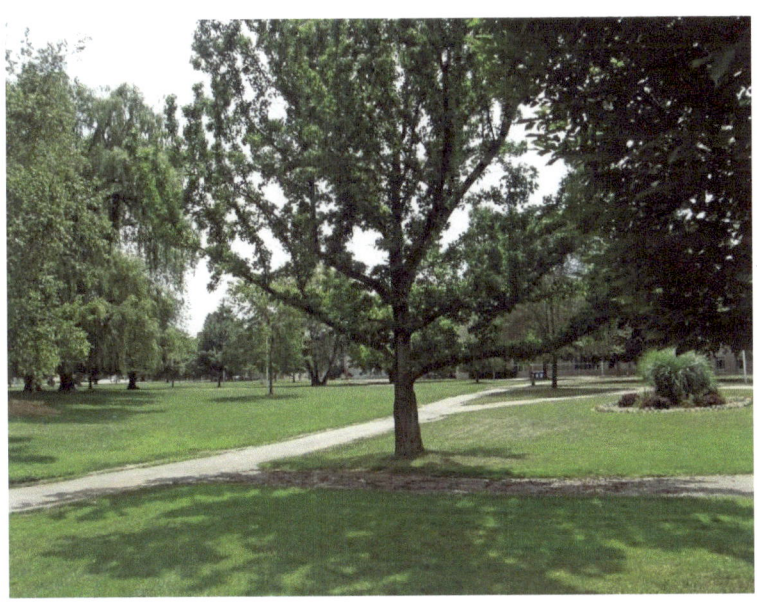

McMaster Divinity College - 1959

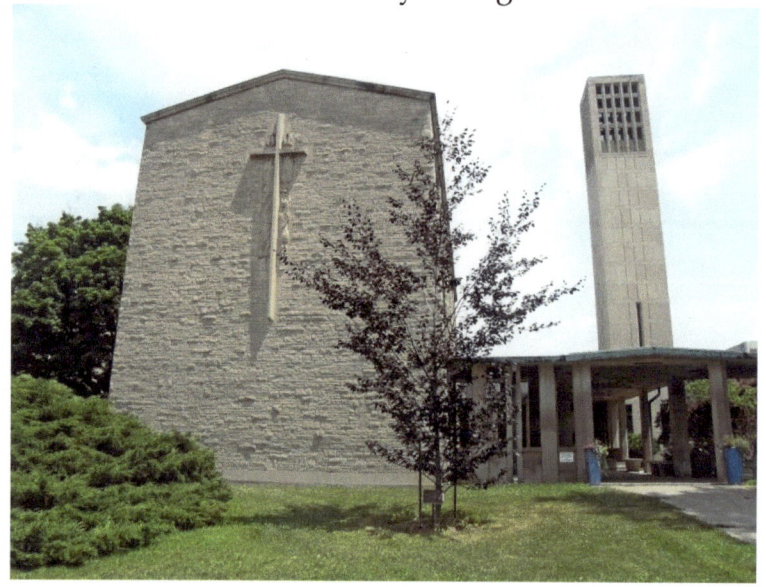

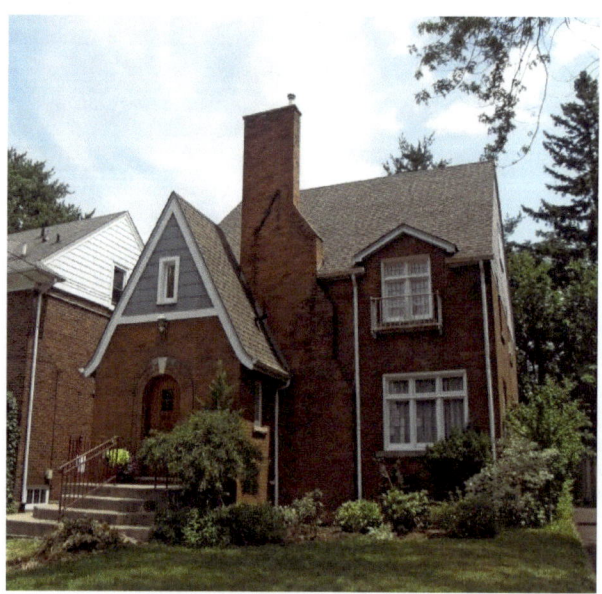

46 Forsyth Avenue North

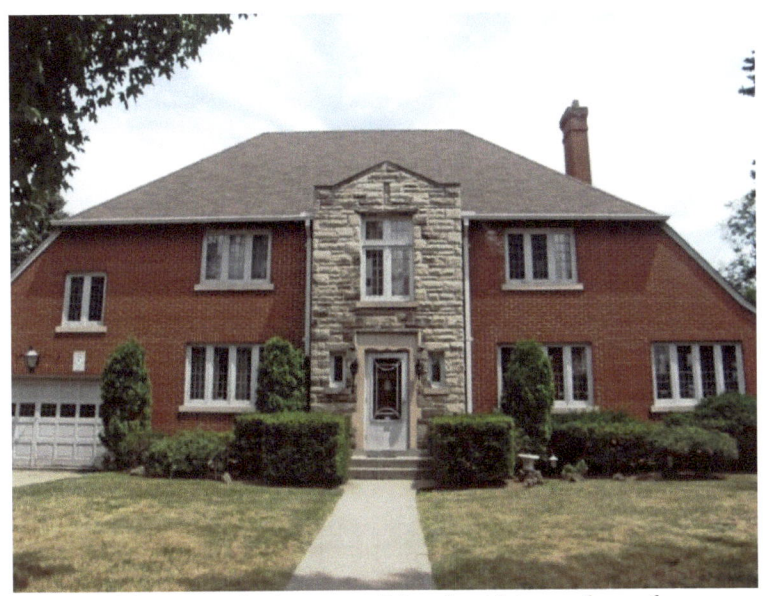

83 Forsyth Avenue North – hipped roof

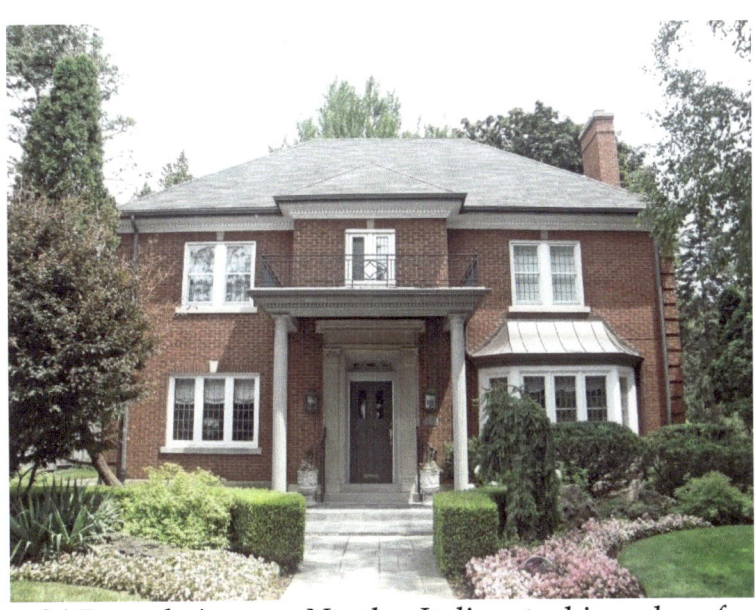

96 Forsyth Avenue North – Italianate, hipped roof

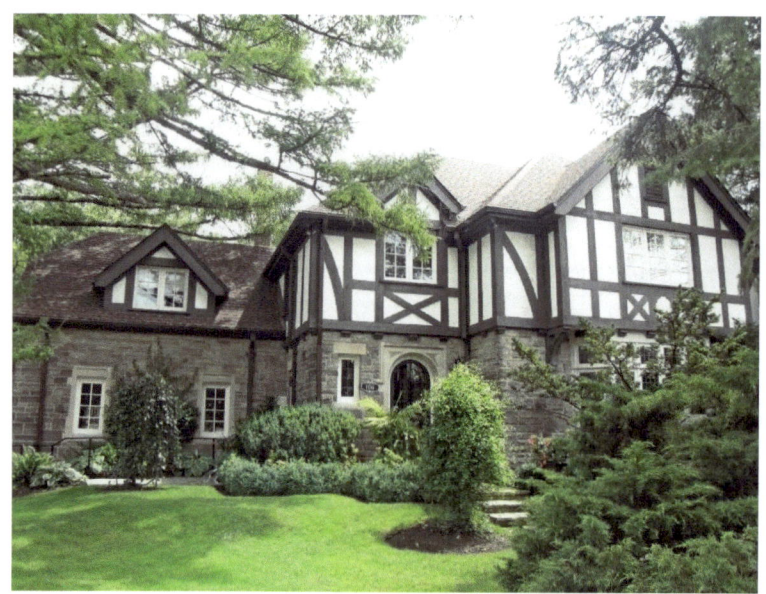

106 Forsyth Avenue North – Tudor style

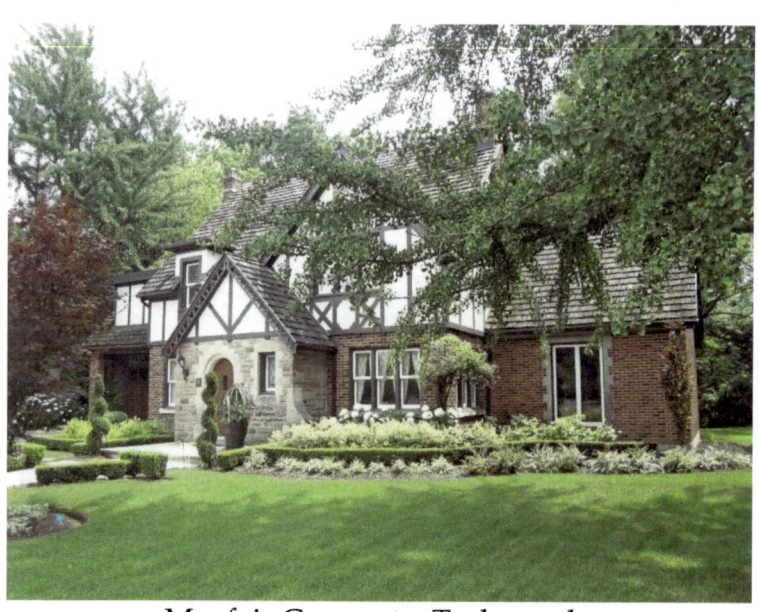

Mayfair Crescent – Tudor style

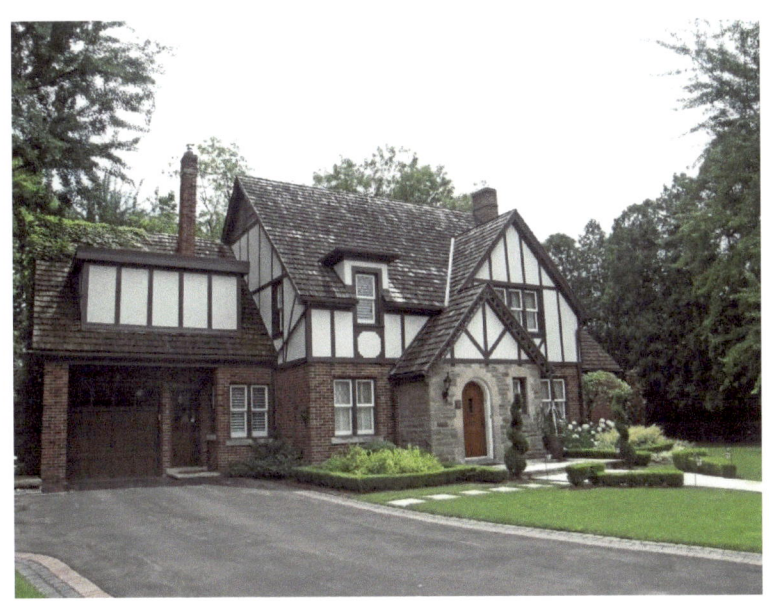

8 Mayfair Crescent – Tudor style

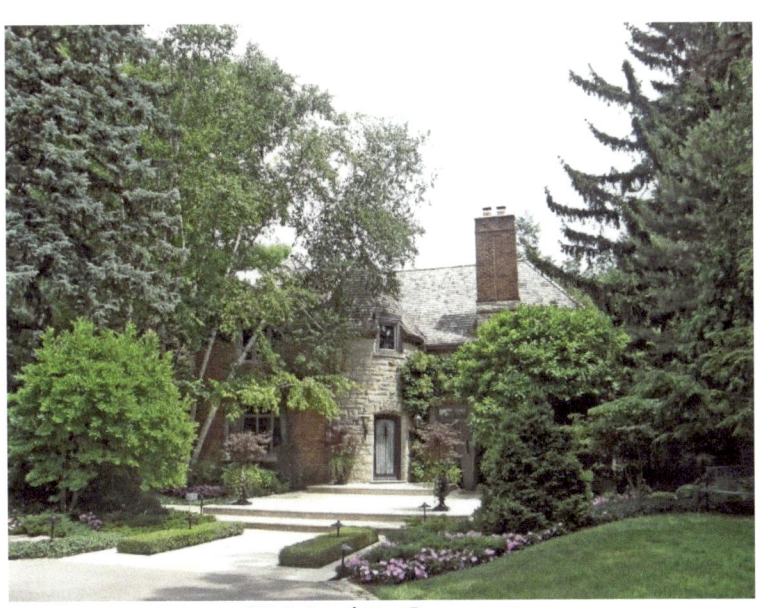

88 Mayfair Crescent

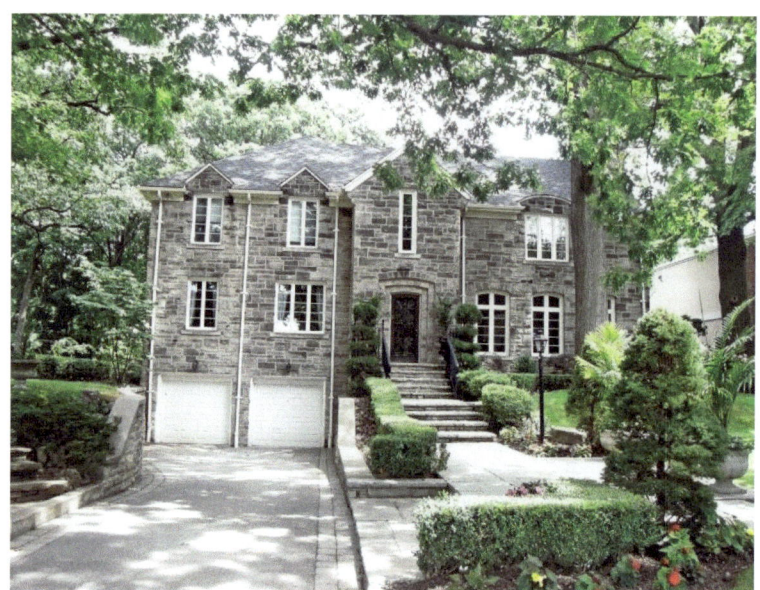

Mayfair Crescent

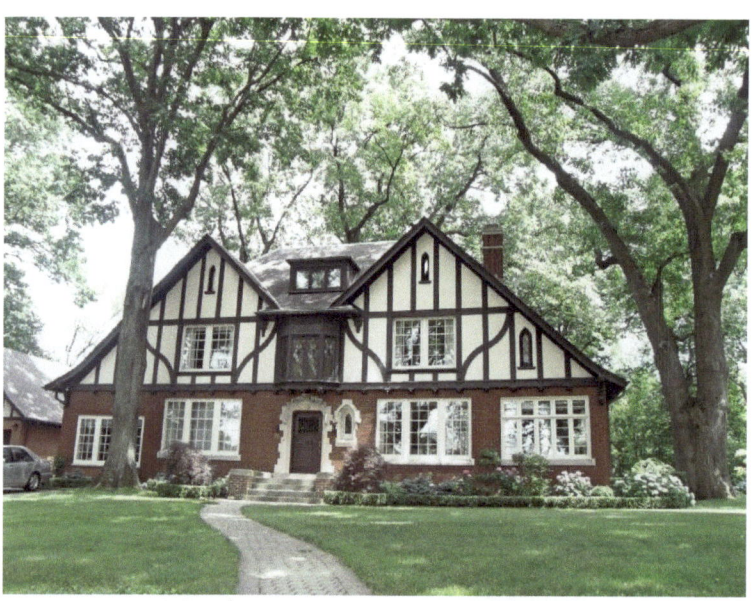

Mayfair Crescent – Tudor style

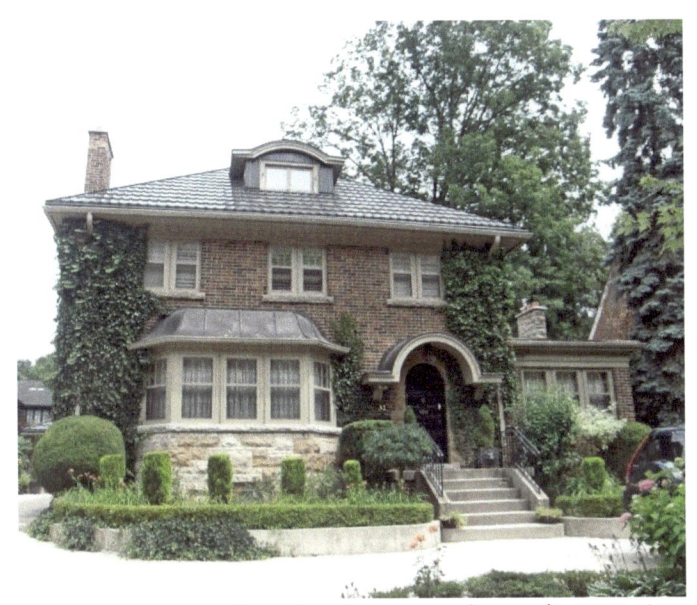

32 Forsyth Avenue South – bay window, dormer in attic

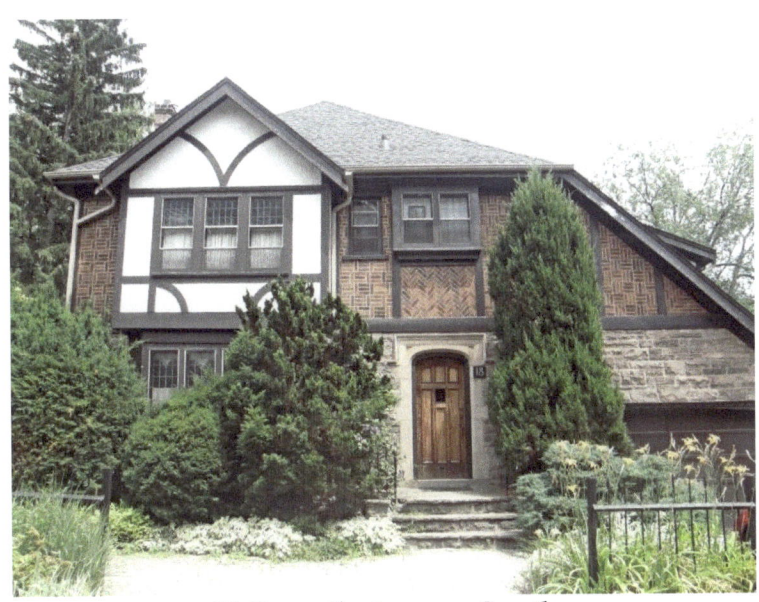

18 Forsyth Avenue South

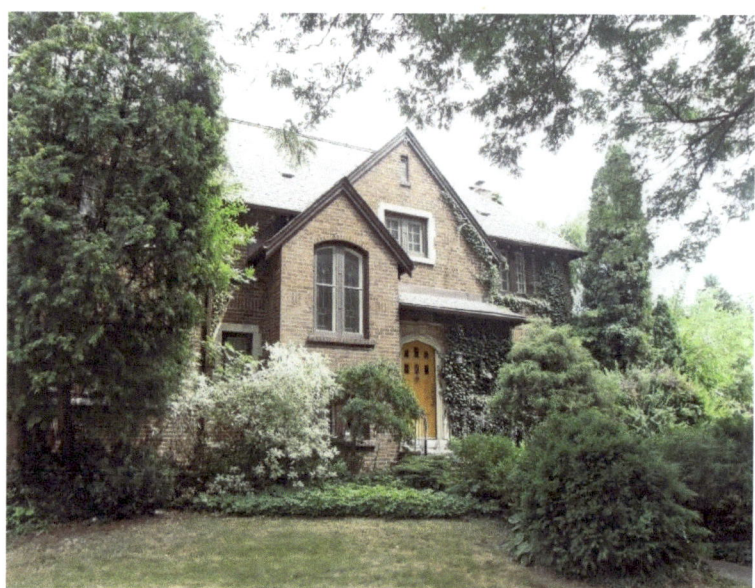

Forsyth Avenue South

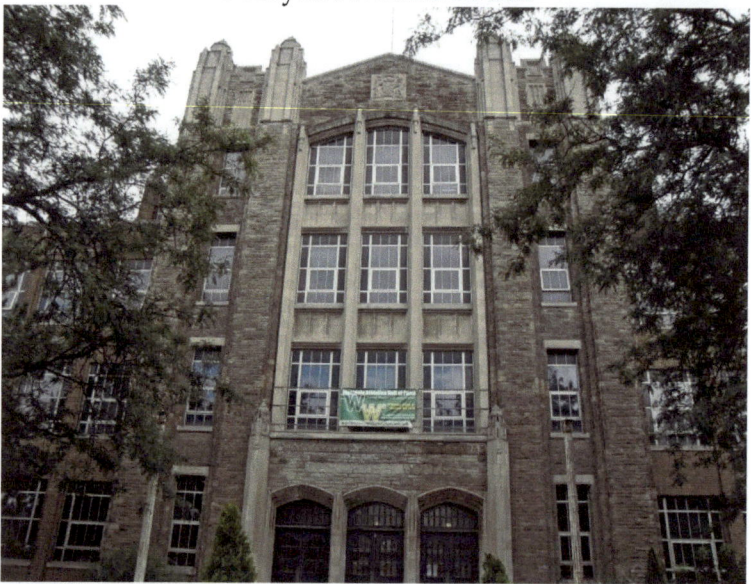

Westdale Secondary School - The entrance has three segmental arches with large stone moulding. The paired piers have ornate finials, giving the impression of weight and stability.

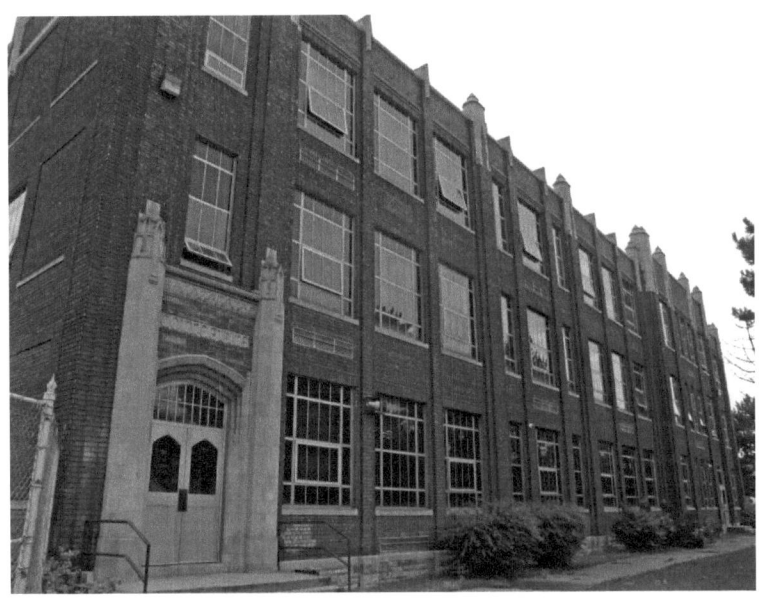

Main Street West - Westdale Secondary School has Neo-Gothic detailing on the portal, on the gable, and on the piers that form the frontispiece. The frontispiece forms a unified and impressive scholarly entrance.

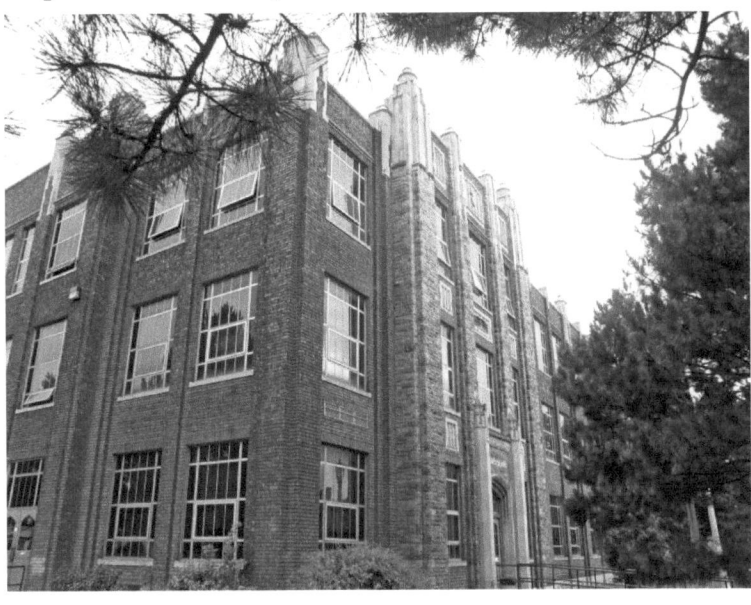

School buildings prior to 1970 usually had more windows than wall. The mullions are strong, and the vertical accents are reminiscent of Gothic cathedral design. Between the window bands are carved spandrels. The muntin bars are pronounced.

Hunter Street West

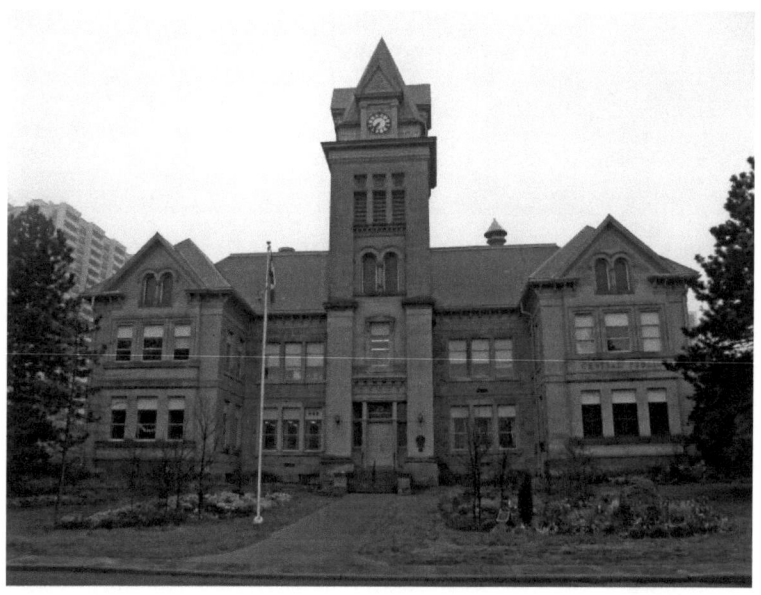

Hamilton Central Public School, built to accommodate 1,000 students, was the largest graded school in Upper Canada and was the only public school in Hamilton when it opened in 1853. The building's original finely proportioned Classical style was extensively remodeled in 1890 with a steeply pitched roof, round-arched windows and a higher central tower to conform to late Victorian tastes.

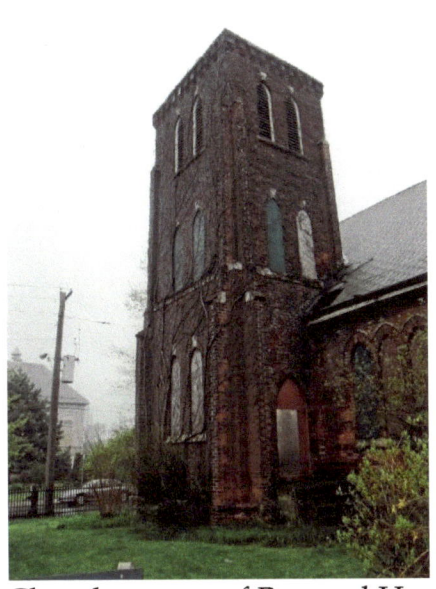

St. Mark's Church, corner of Bay and Hunter Streets
Built in 1877 - It was the first Anglican Church in Hamilton to
be built of brick.

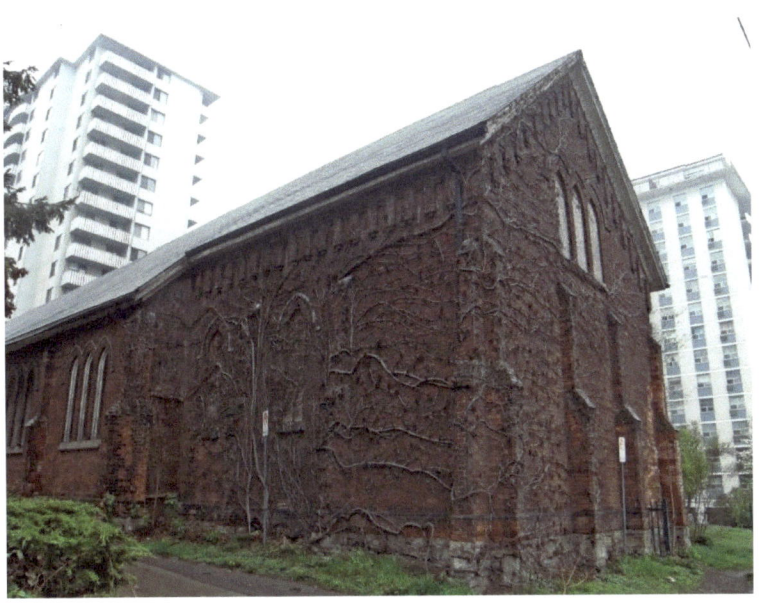

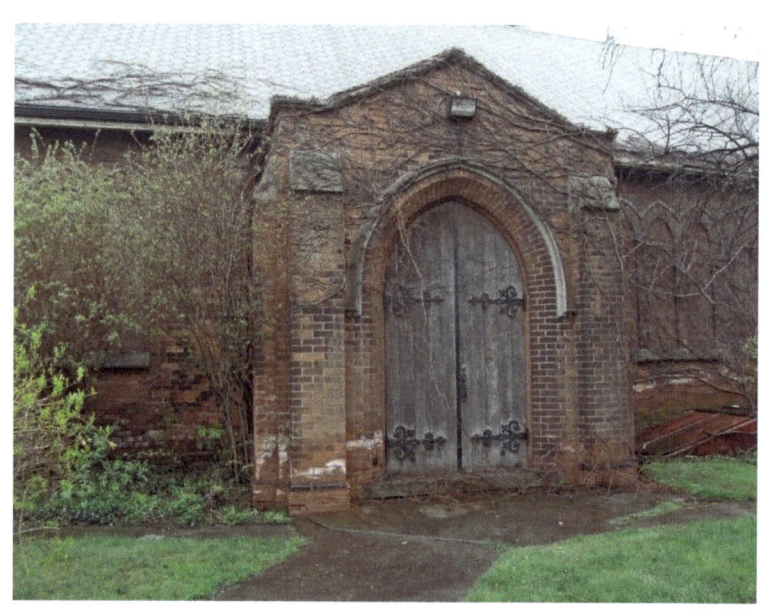

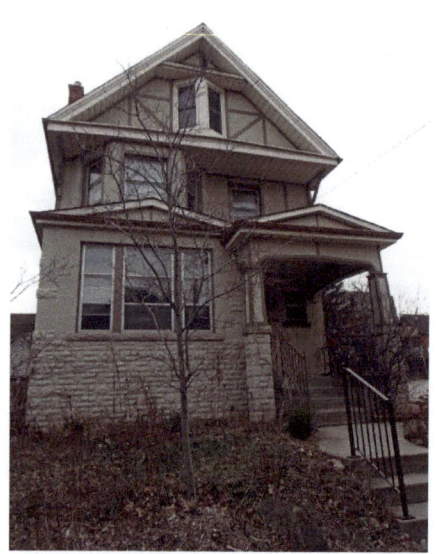

99 Stanley Avenue Edwardian, pediments

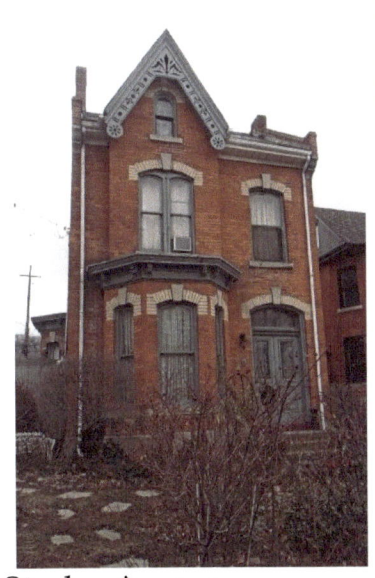

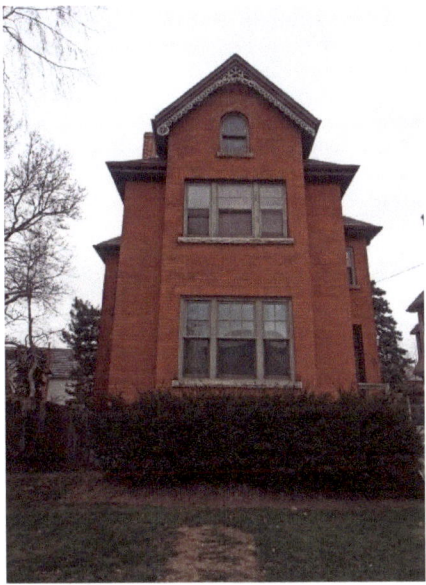

1 Stanley Avenue
Gothic Revival, bay window,
arched window voussoirs
and keystones, verge board trim

46 Stanley Avenue

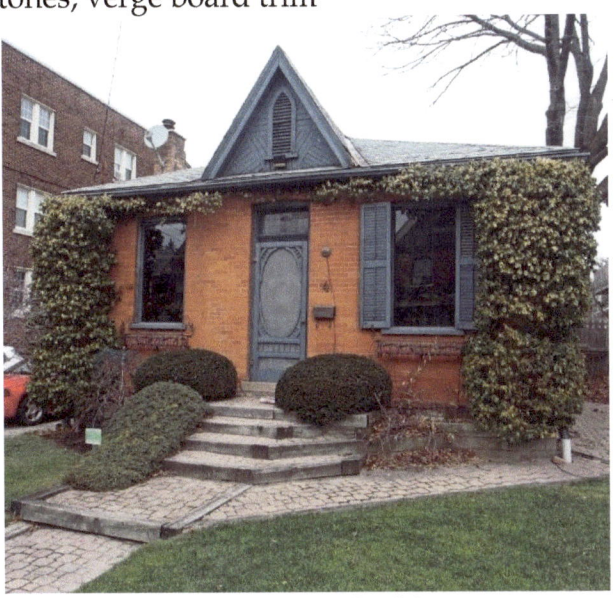

4 Stanley Avenue – Gothic cottage

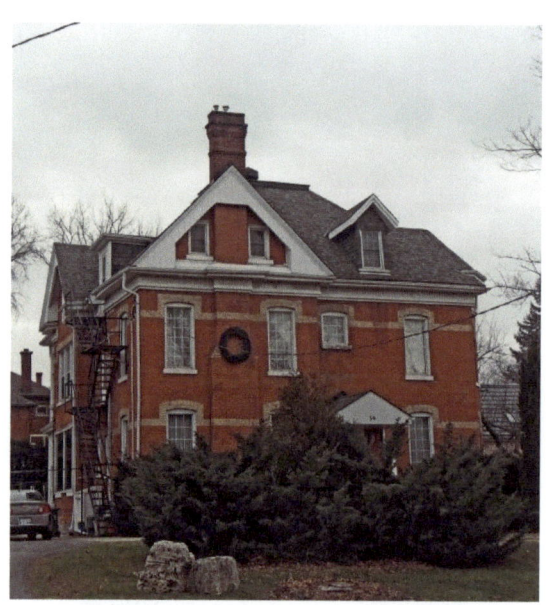

39 Stanley Avenue - banding

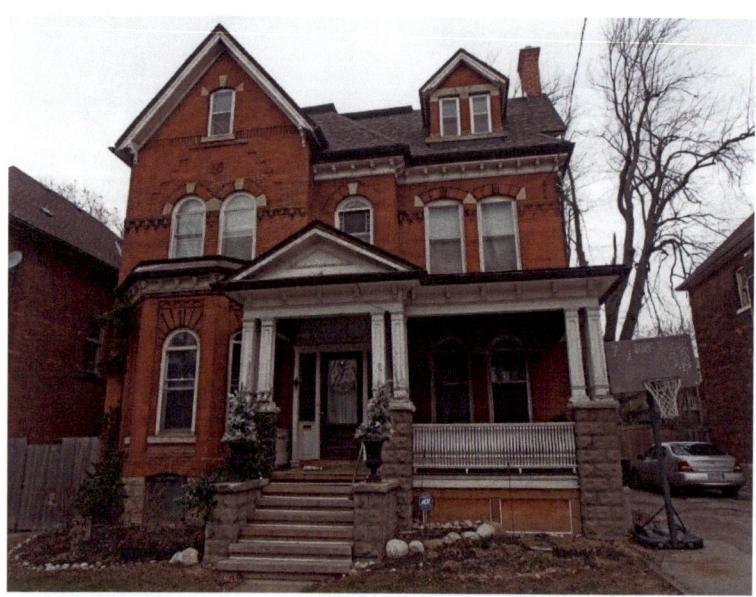

Stanley Avenue – corbelled dentils, dormer, bay window, pediment, arched window voussoirs with keystones

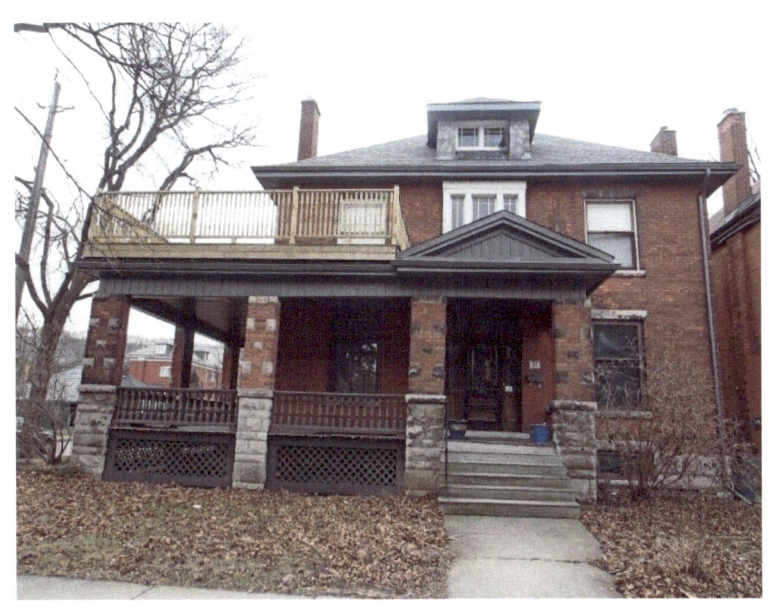

55 Stanley Avenue, dormer, pediment, wraparound verandah

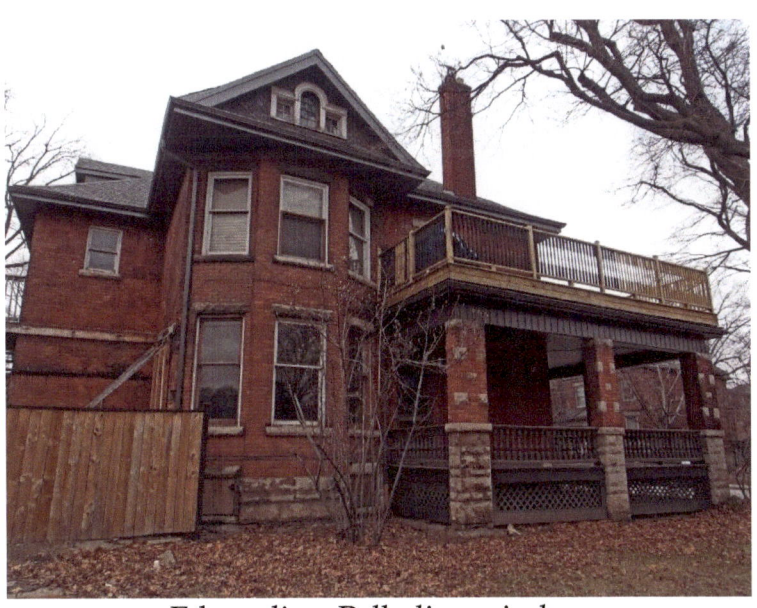

Edwardian, Palladian window

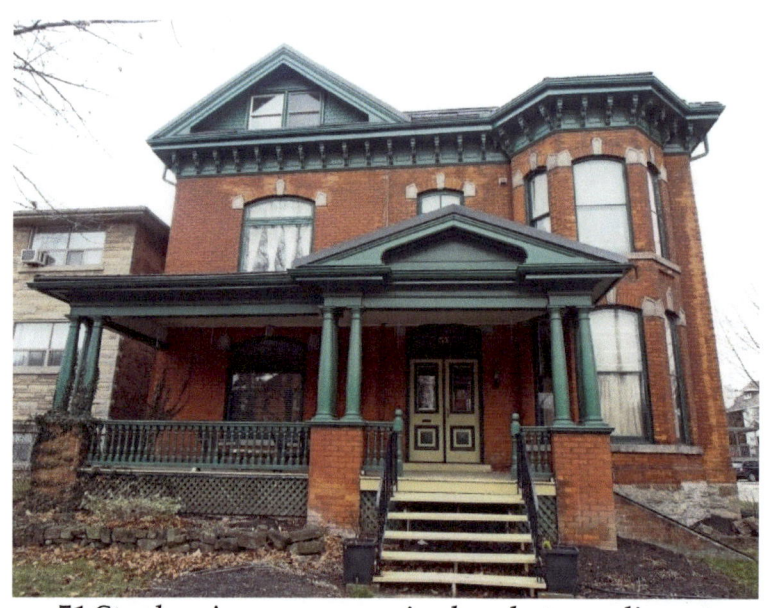

51 Stanley Avenue – cornice brackets, pediment

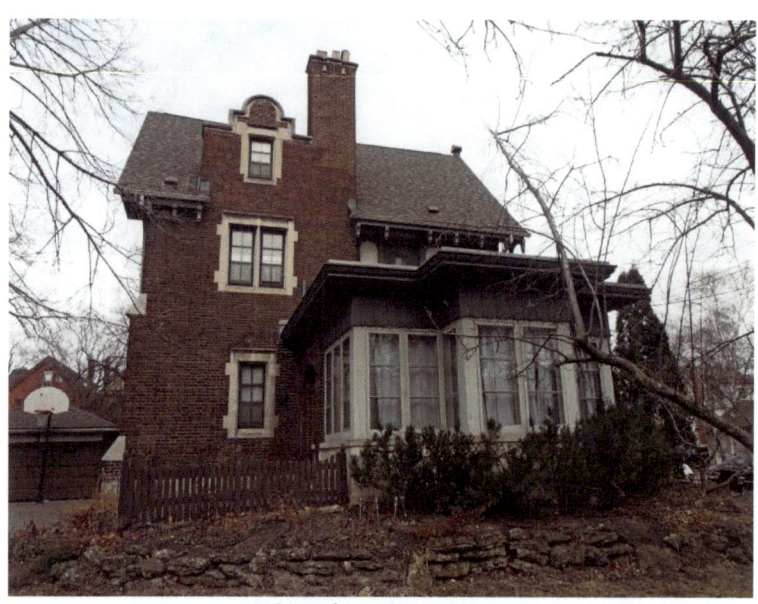

Stanley Avenue

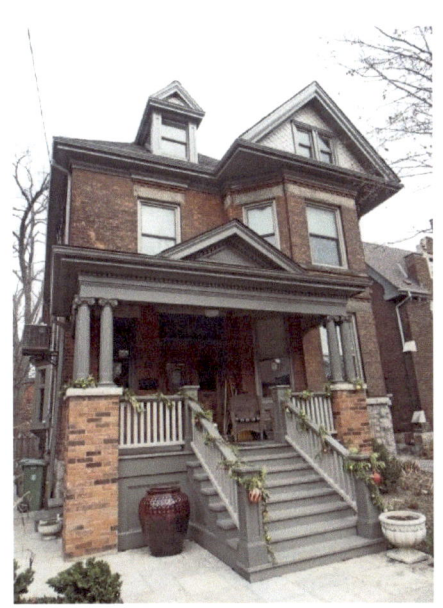

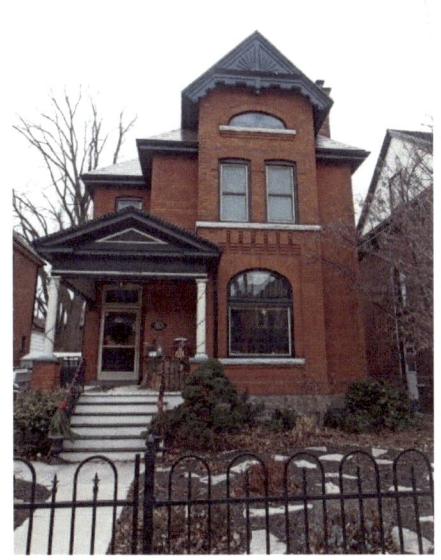

60 Stanley Avenue
Dormer

61 Stanley Avenue
verge board trim on gable

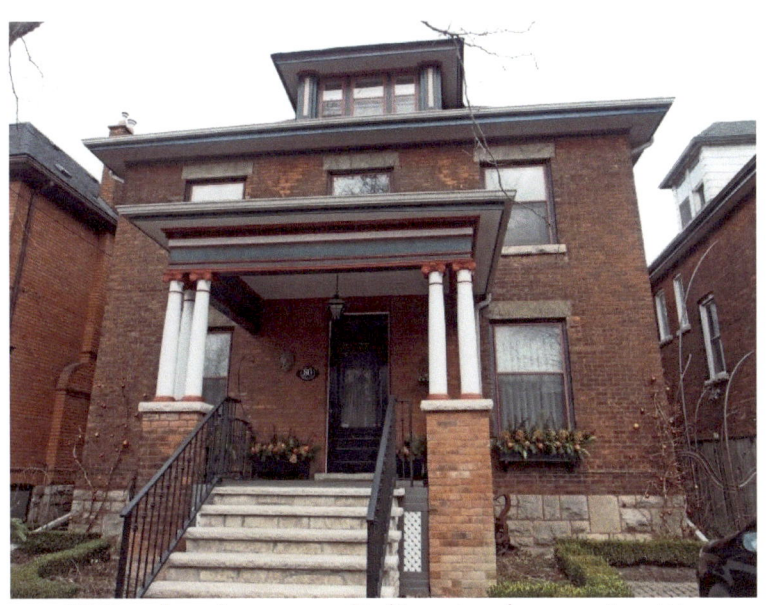

80 Stanley Avenue – Italianate, dormer in attic,
pillars with Ionic capitals

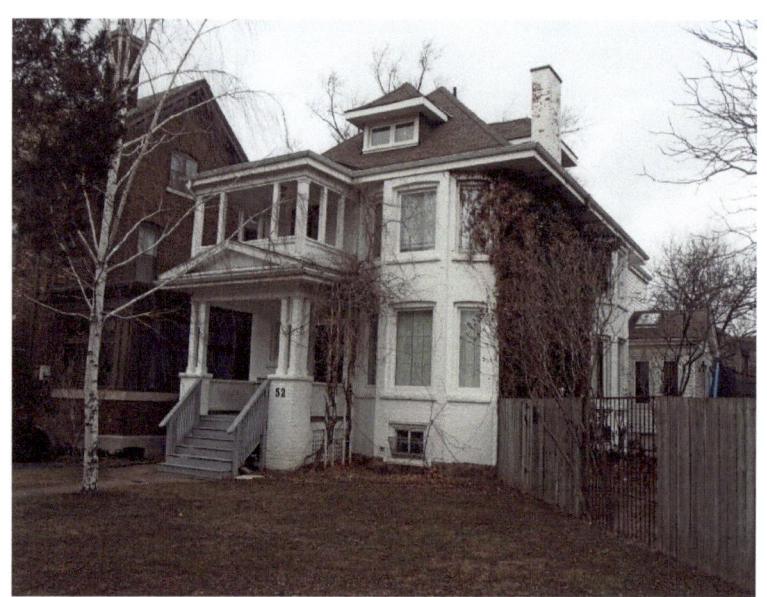

52 Homewood Avenue - dormer

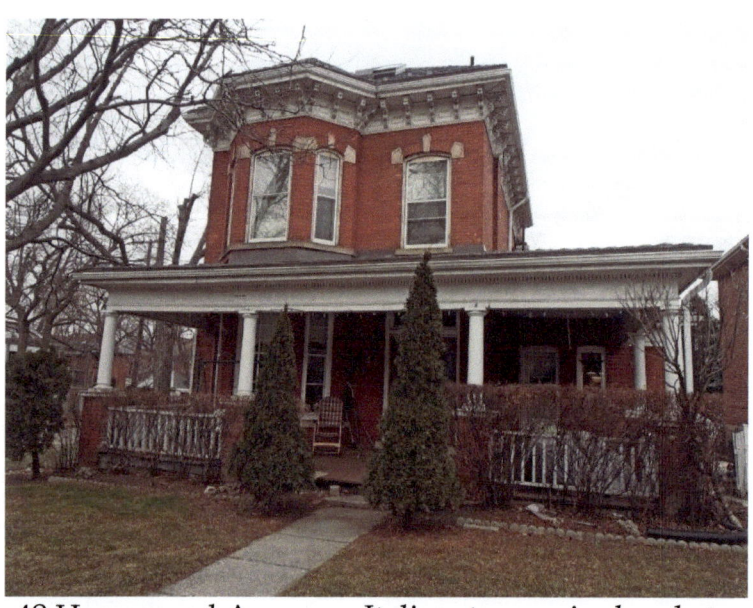

48 Homewood Avenue – Italianate, cornice brackets,
Two-storey bay window

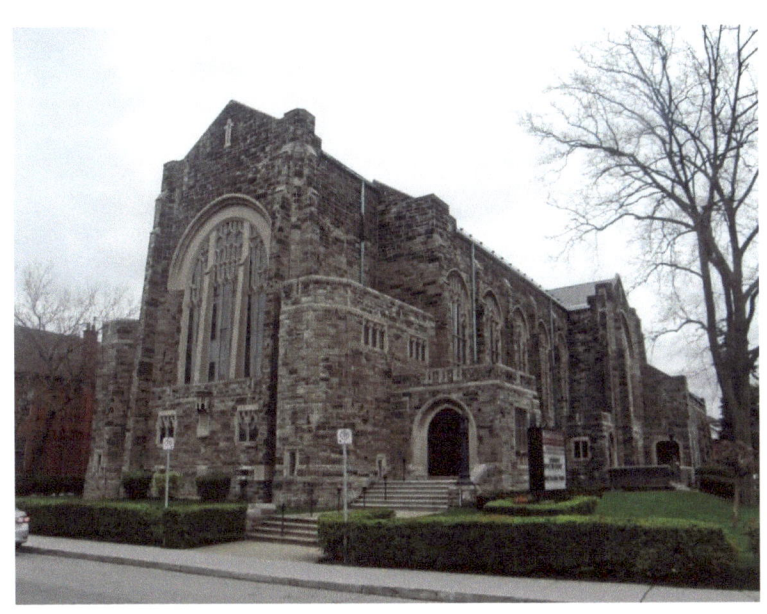

Melrose United Church - 1928

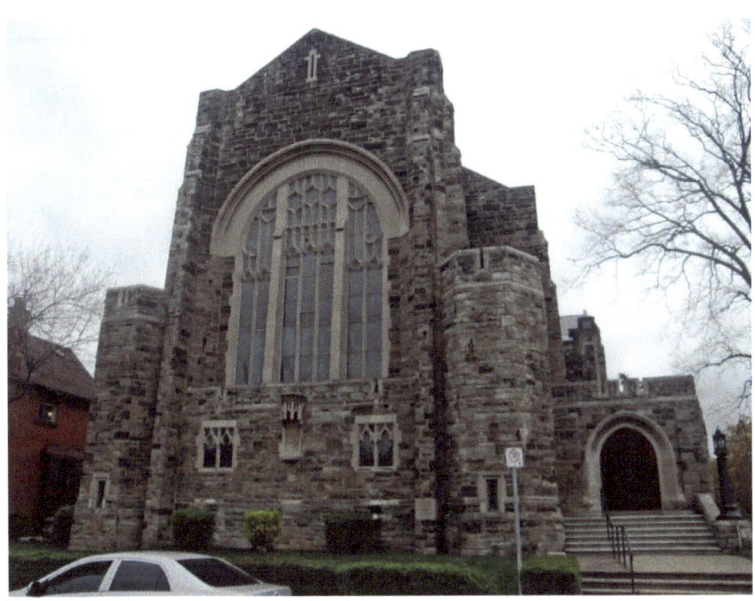

86 Homewood Avenue

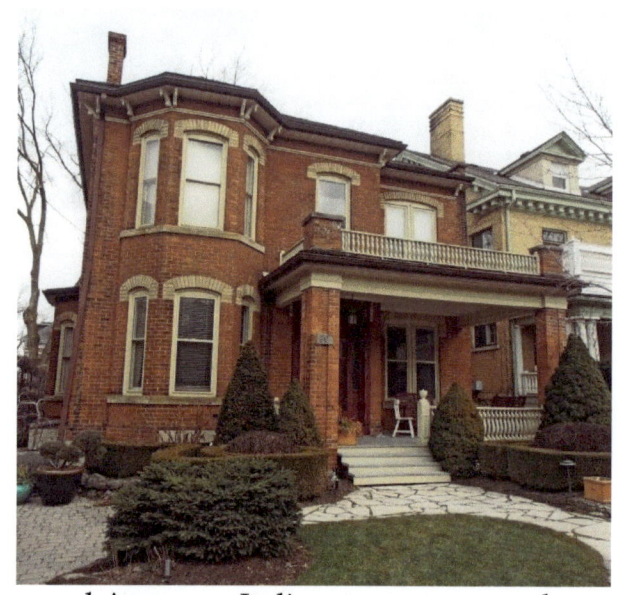

30 Homewood Avenue – Italianate, two-storey bay windows, balcony above verandah, arched window voussoirs

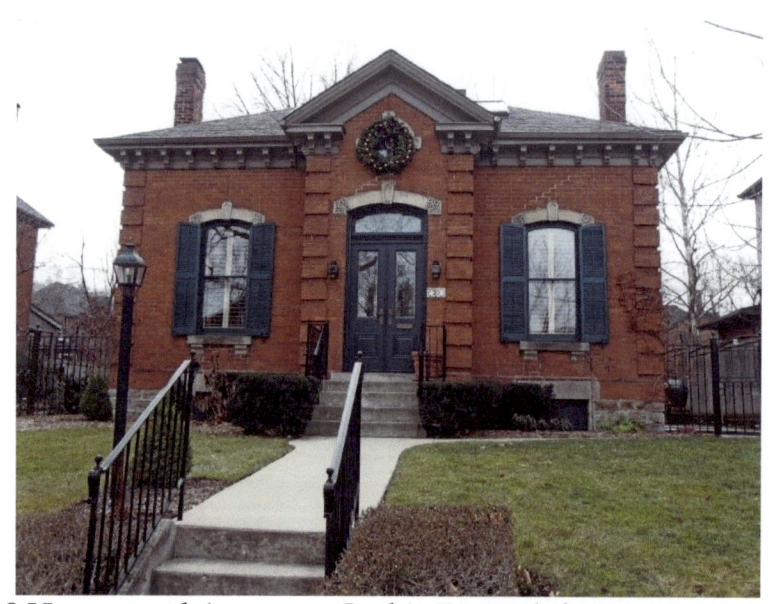

39 Homewood Avenue – Gothic Revival, frontispiece with cornice return on gable, corner quoins, cornice brackets

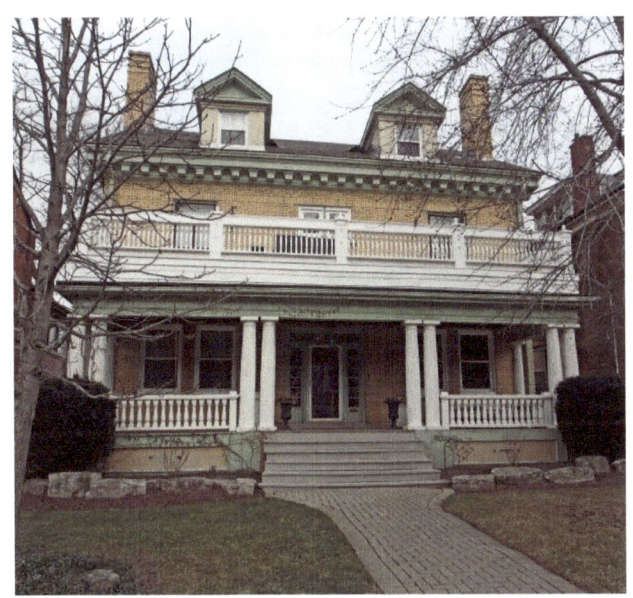

26 Homewood Avenue – Italianate, dormers,
balcony full-width of second floor

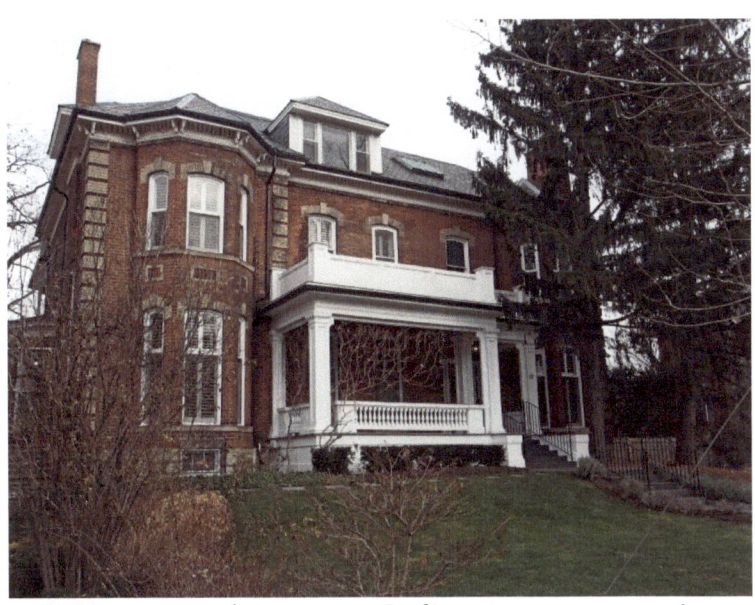

22 Homewood Avenue – Italianate, corner quoins,
cornice brackets, two-storey bay window, keystones

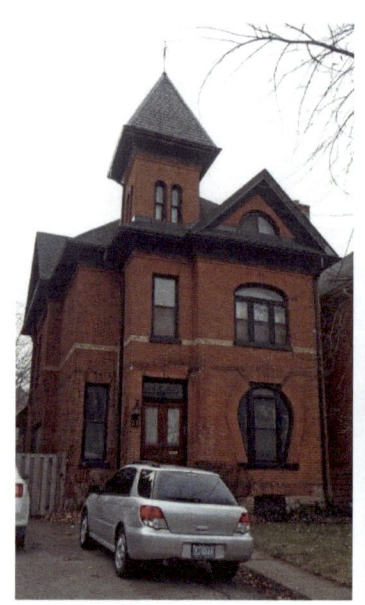
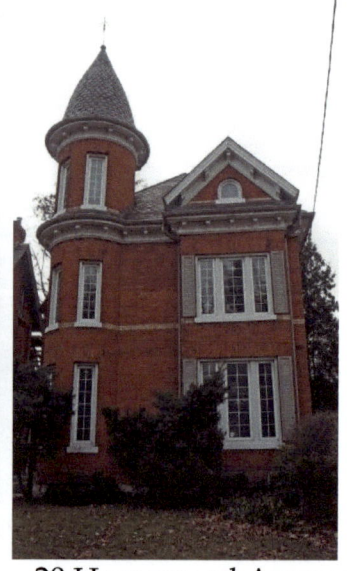

21 Homewood Avenue   20 Homewood Avenue

Queen Anne style, turrets

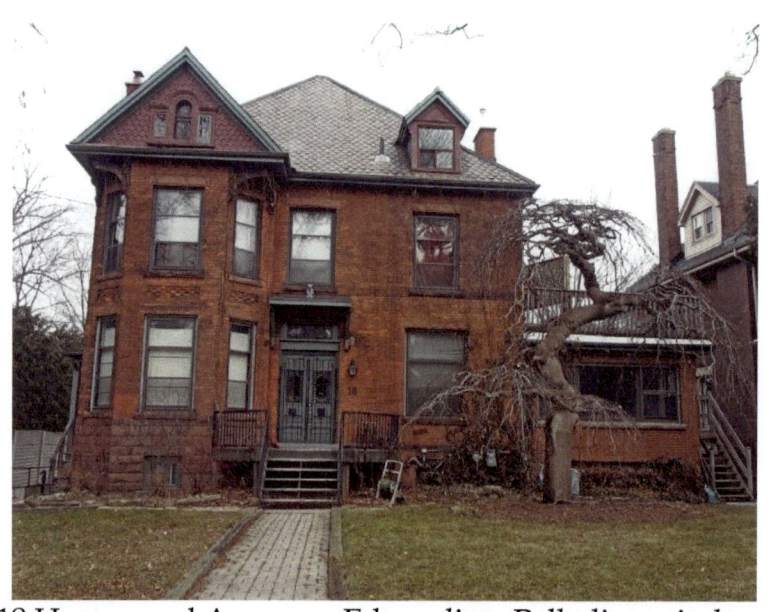

18 Homewood Avenue – Edwardian, Palladian window, dormer, fretwork under cornice

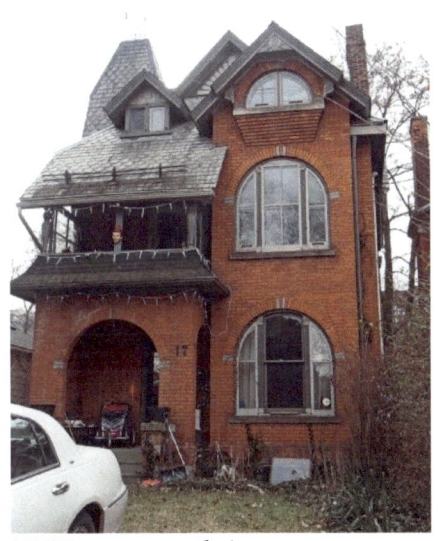

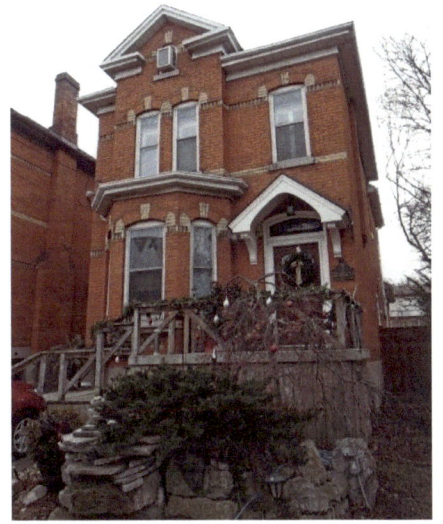

17 Homewood Avenue
Queen Anne Style

7 Homewood Avenue
Italianate, bay window,
cornice return on gable

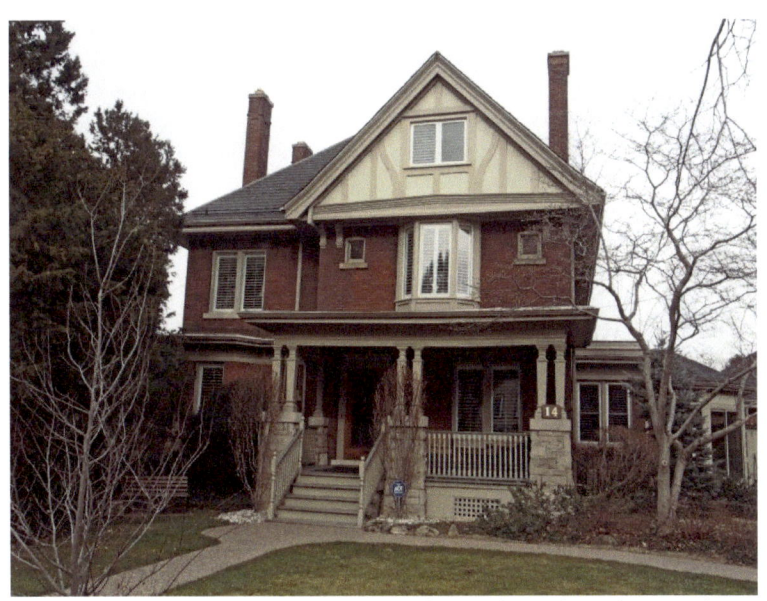

14 Homewood Avenue – Edwardian/Tudor style

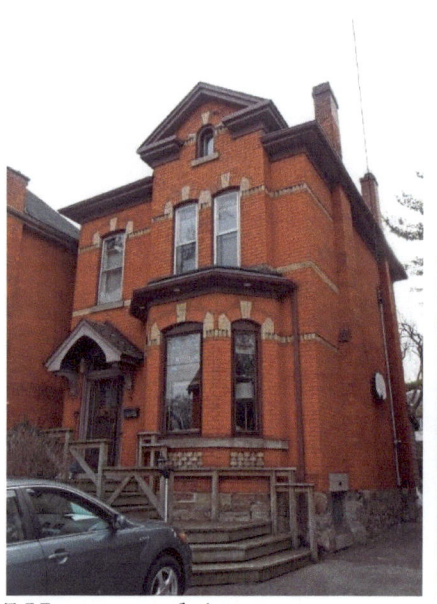

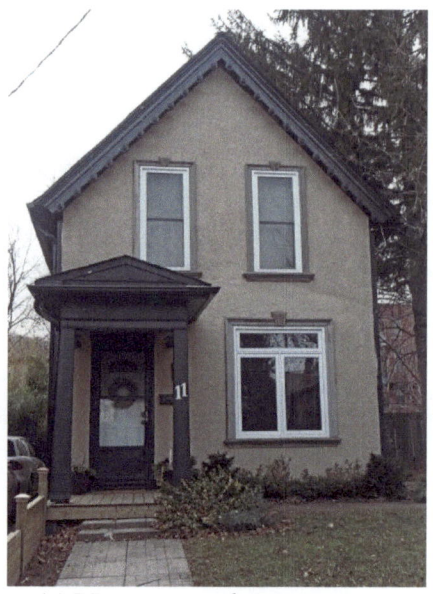

5 Homewood Avenue
Italianate, bay window
Banding, dichromatic

11 Homewood Avenue
Gothic Revival, stucco
pediment above porch

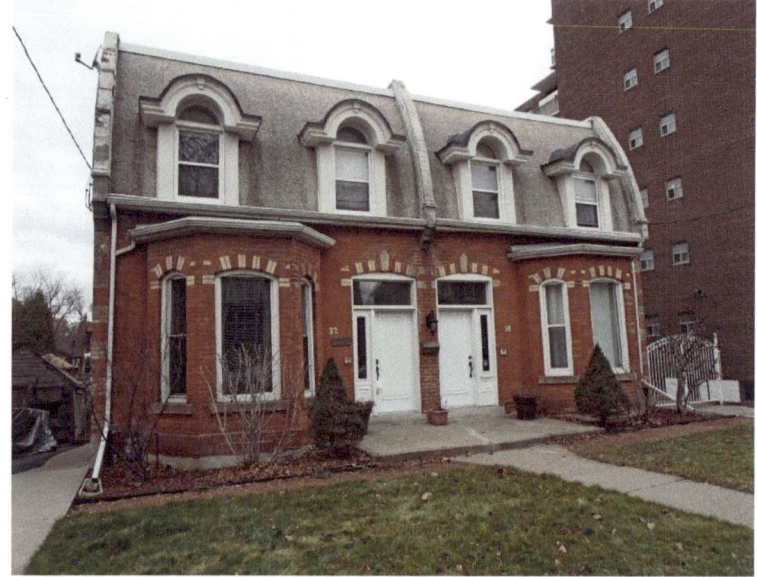

30-32 Erie Avenue – Second Empire, mansard roof, dormers with
window hoods, dichromatic brickwork
Unit 32 Harry A. Ellis, Draftsman

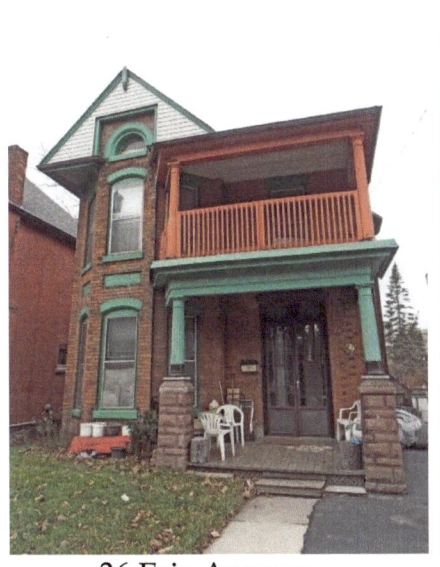

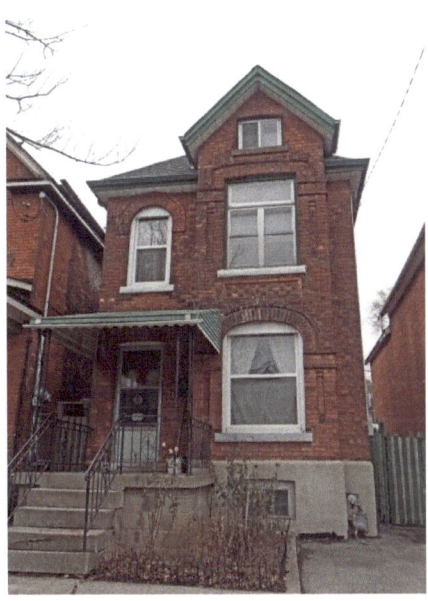

36 Erie Avenue
2½-storey tower-like bay

35 Erie Avenue
2½-storey frontispiece

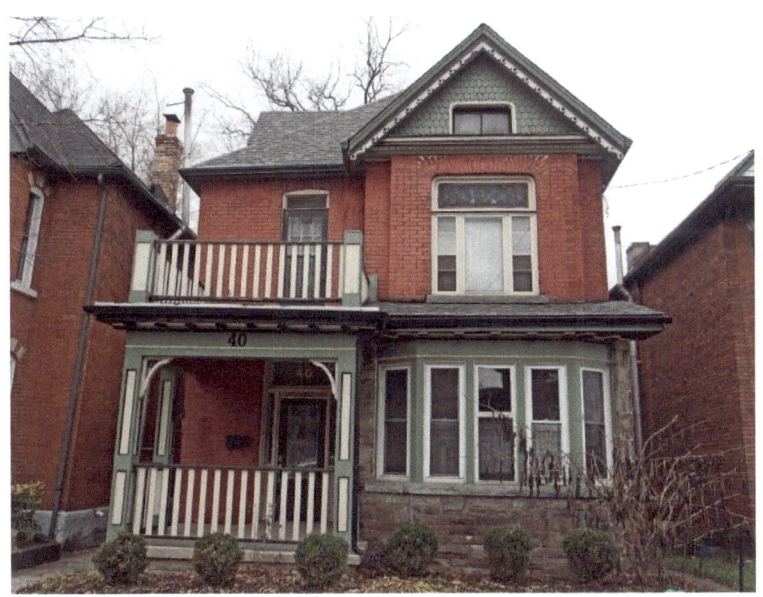

40 Erie Avenue – Edwardian, balcony, bay window

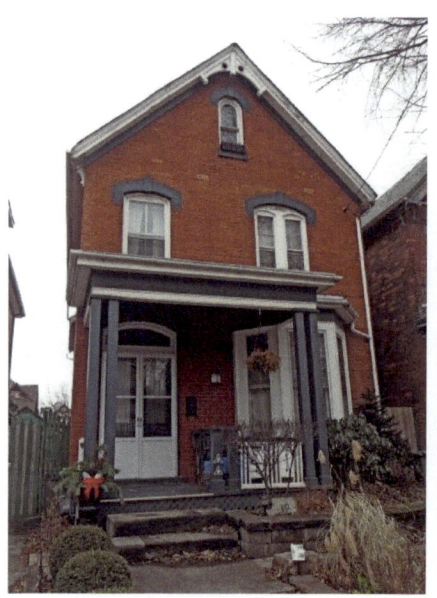

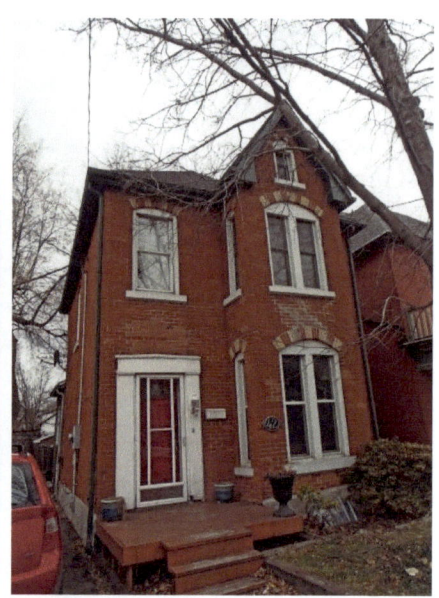

39 Erie Avenue
Gothic Revival

42 Erie Avenue

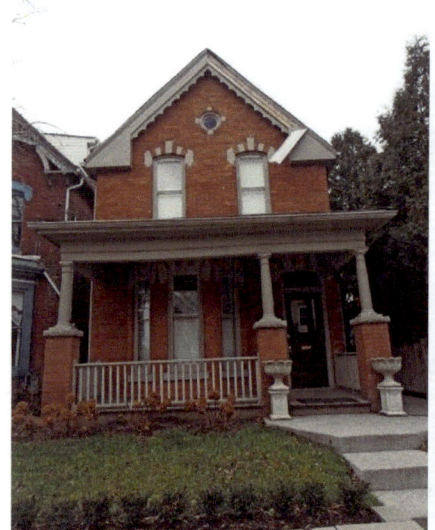

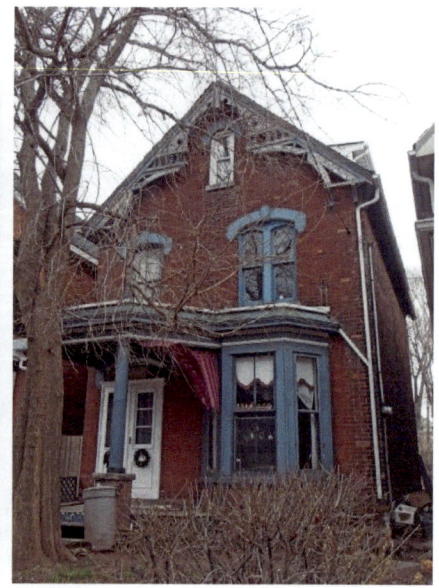

Erie Avenue
Gothic Revival, verge board trim

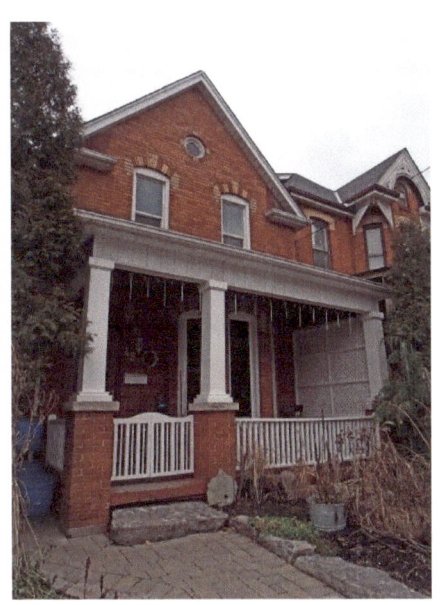
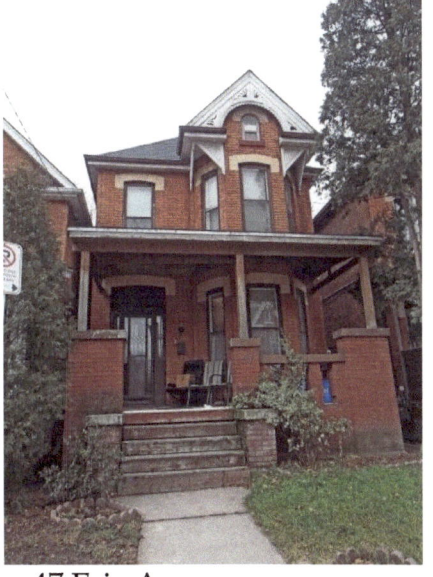

45 Erie Avenue
Gothic Revival

47 Erie Avenue
verge board trim, fretwork

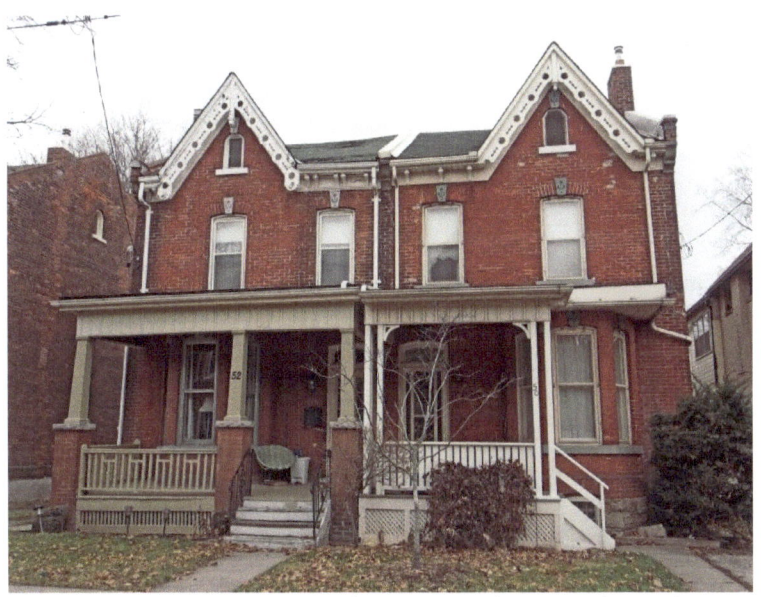

50-52 Erie Avenue – Gothic Revival, verge board trim
on gables, cornice brackets

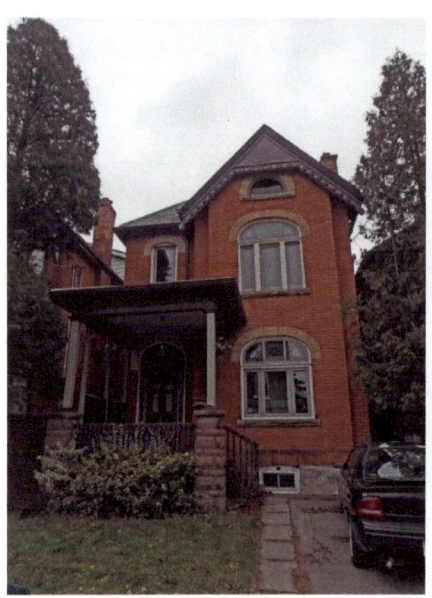

51 Erie Avenue

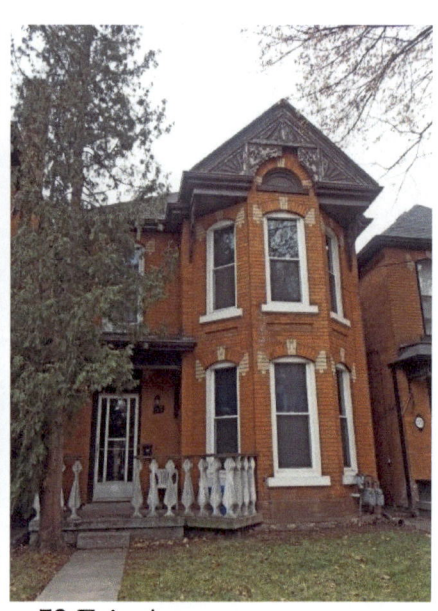

53 Erie Avenue
Verge board, two-storey bay

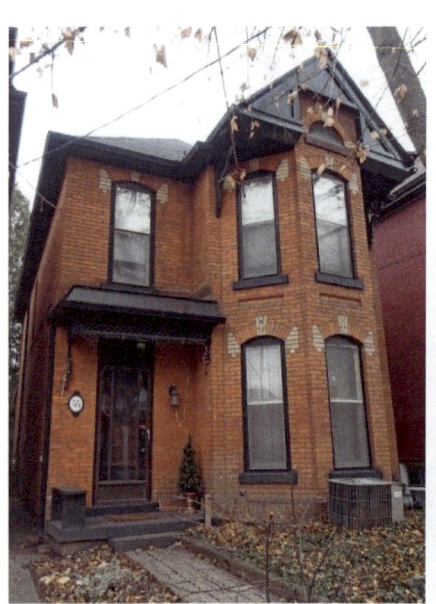

55 Erie Avenue

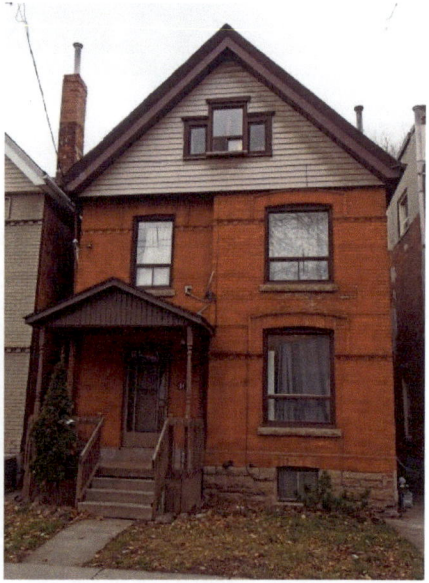

58 Erie Avenue – Edwardian
Palladian window

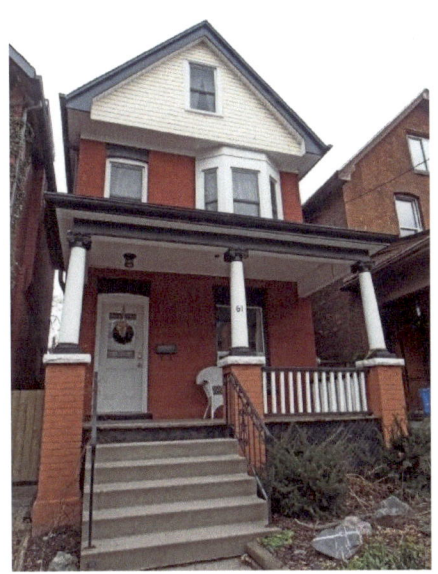

61 Erie Avenue
Edwardian, Ionic capitals

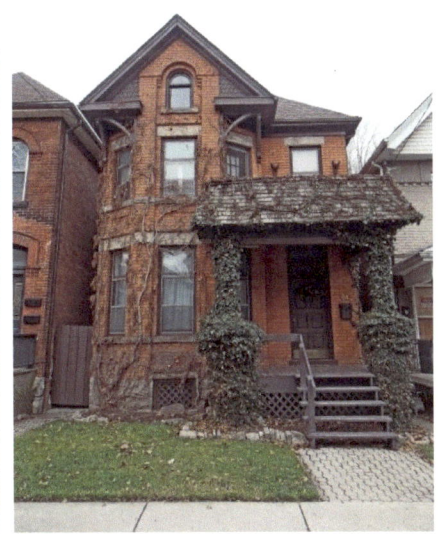

64 Erie Avenue
cornice return on gable

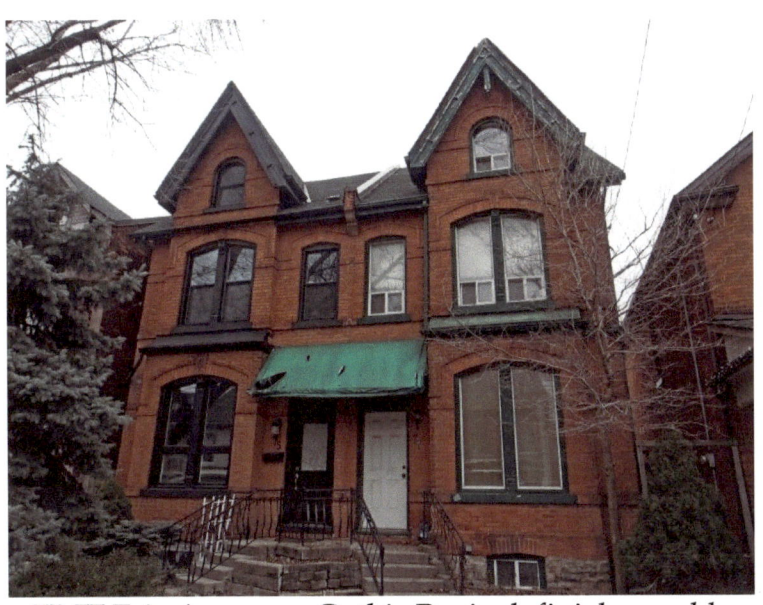

75-77 Erie Avenue – Gothic Revival, finial on gable

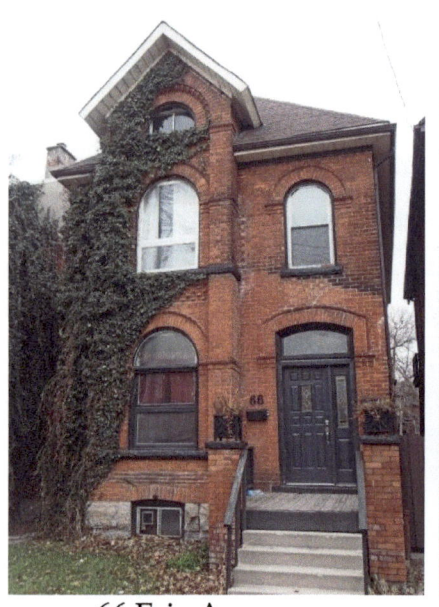

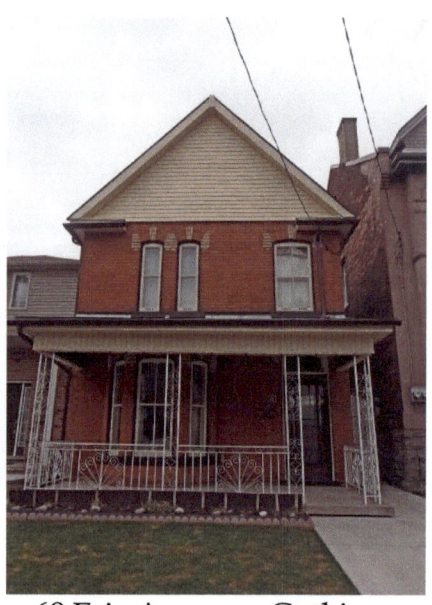

66 Erie Avenue

69 Erie Avenue - Gothic

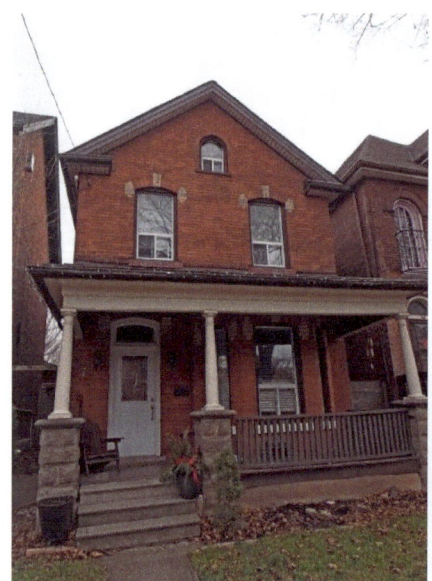

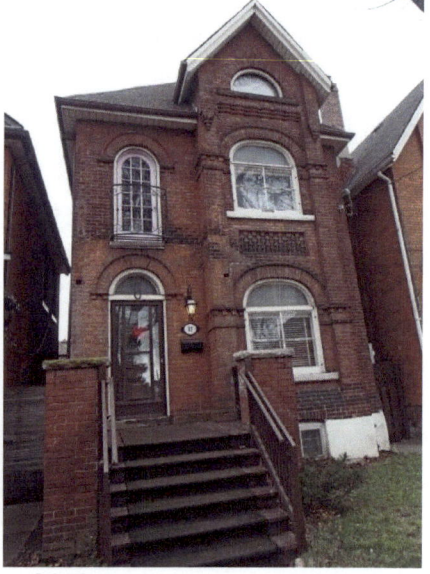

79 Erie Avenue
Gothic – cornice return

81 Erie Avenue
2½-storey tower-like bay
Romanesque style window voussoirs

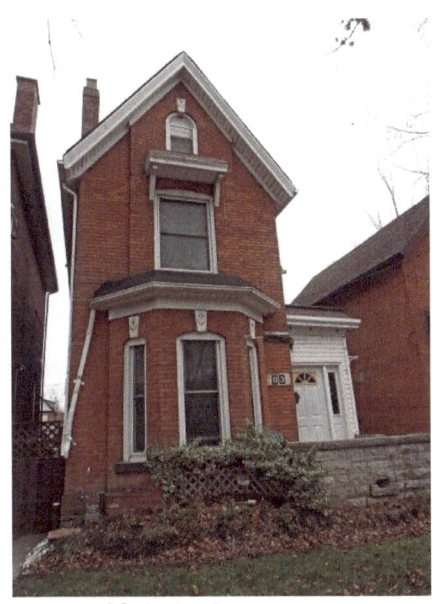 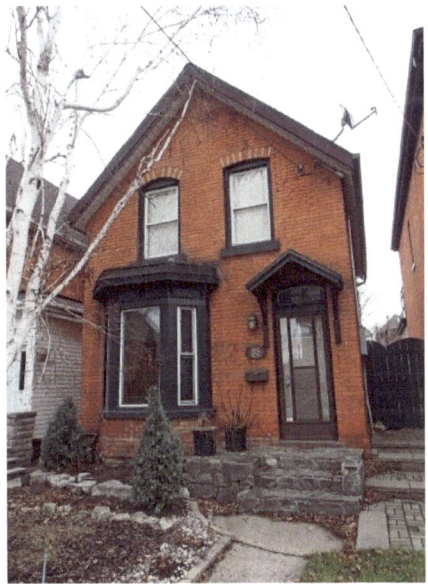

83 Erie Avenue   85 Erie Avenue
Gothic Revival, bay windows
keystones

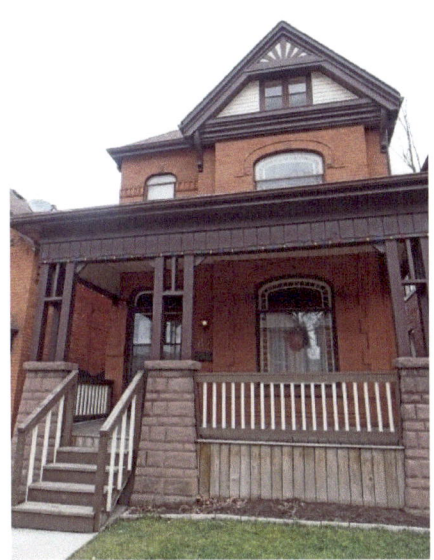 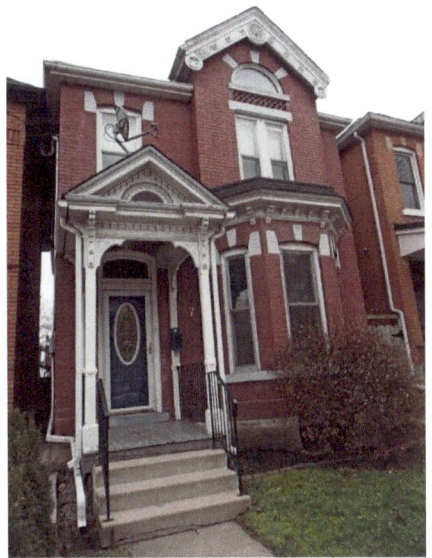

87 Erie Avenue   97 Erie Avenue
Verge board trim, cornice
brackets, pediment with decorated tympanum, keystones

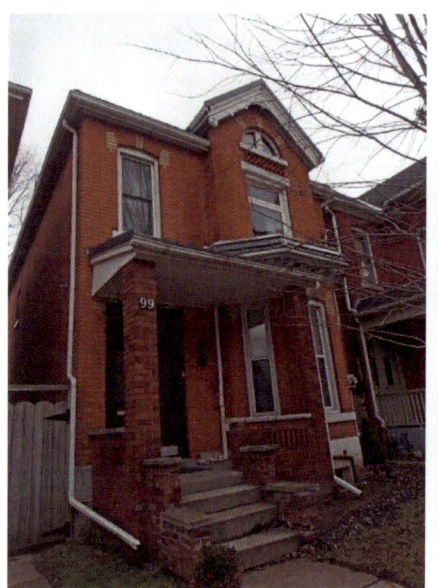

99 Erie Avenue
Verge board time on gable

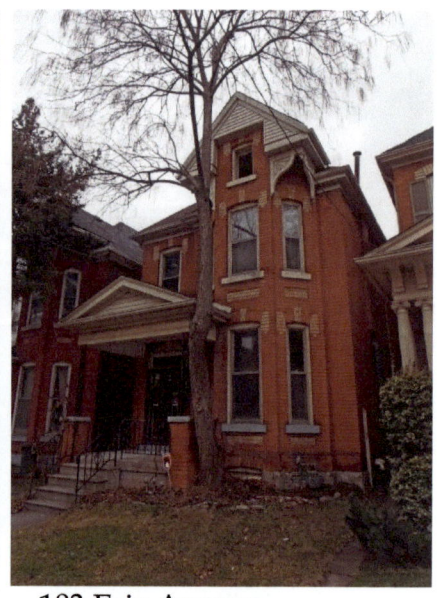

103 Erie Avenue
fretwork, pediment

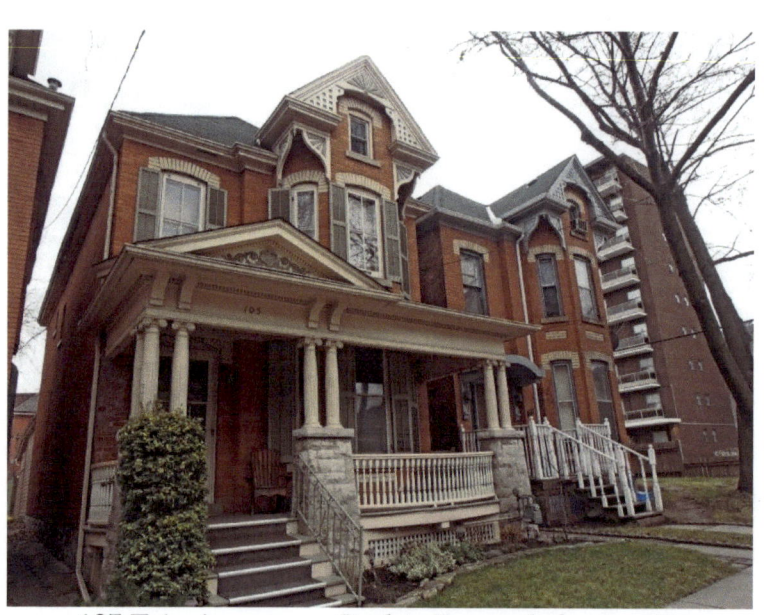

105 Erie Avenue – Gothic Revival, fretwork,
Pediment, Ionic capitals

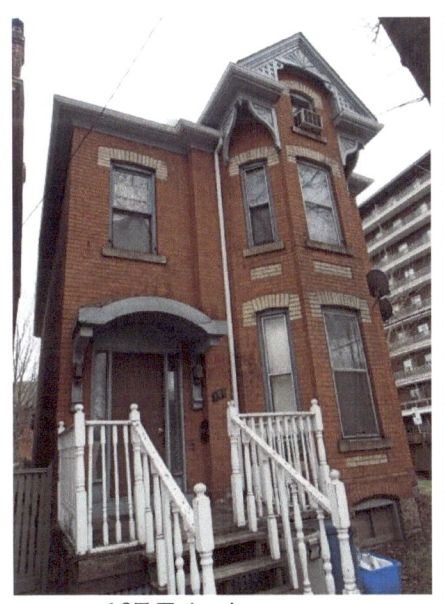

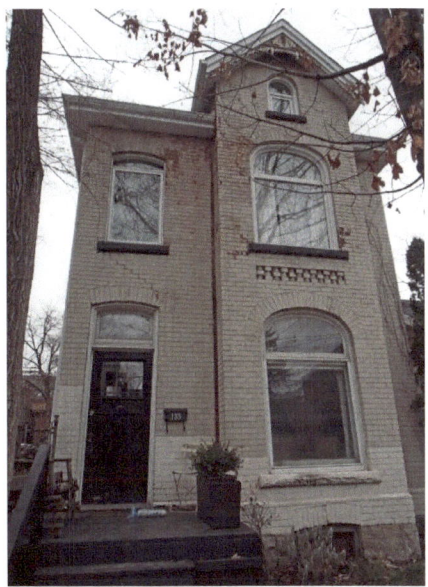

107 Erie Avenue
Fretwork

133 Erie Avenue

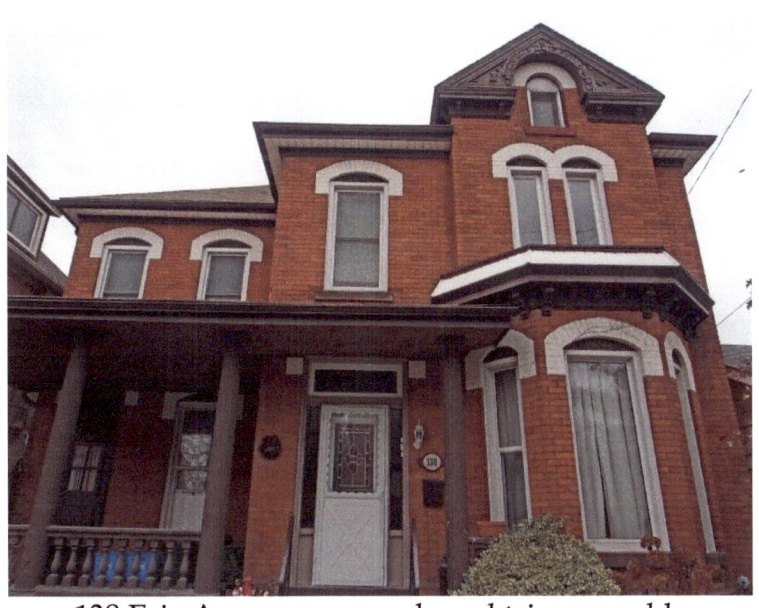

138 Erie Avenue – verge board trim on gable

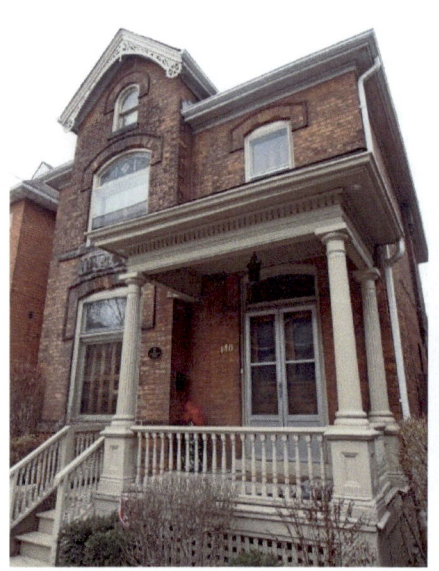

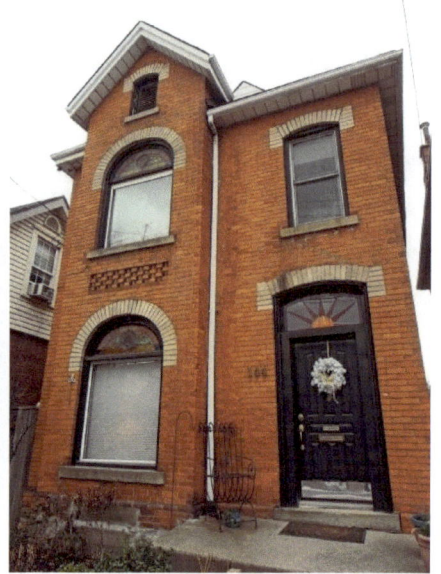

140 Erie Avenue
verge board trim

144 Erie Avenue

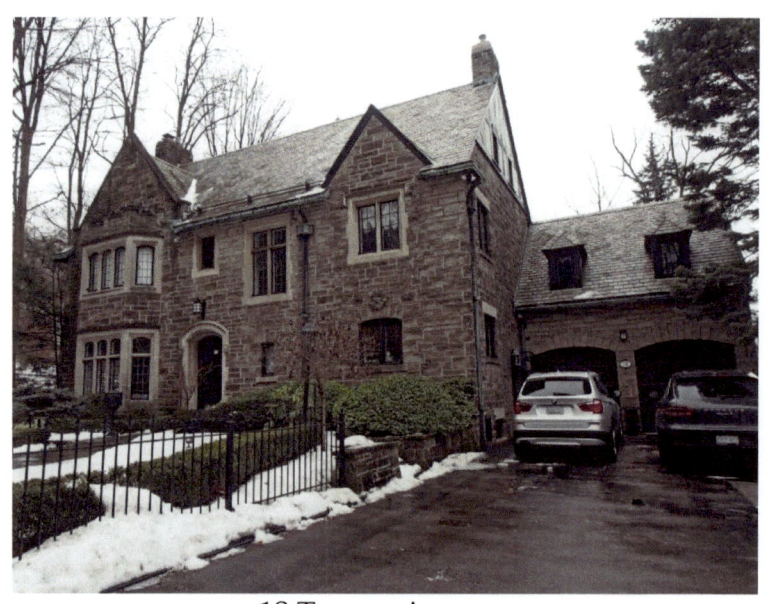

18 Turner Avenue

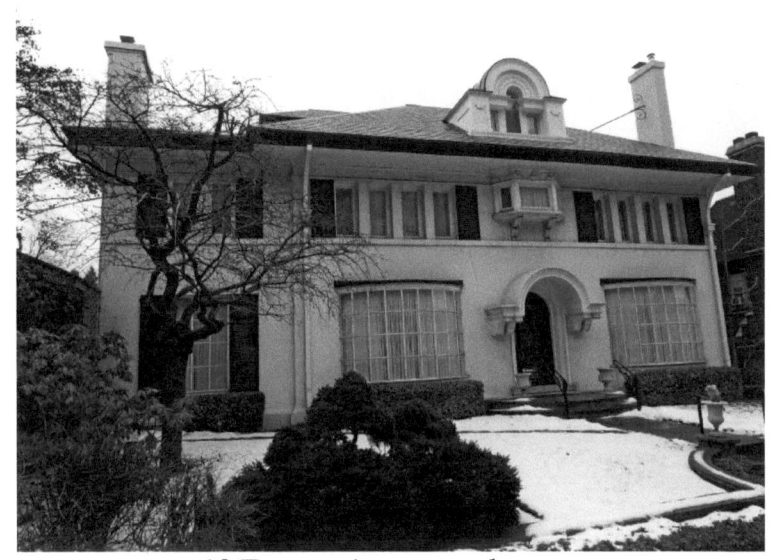

10 Turner Avenue - dormer

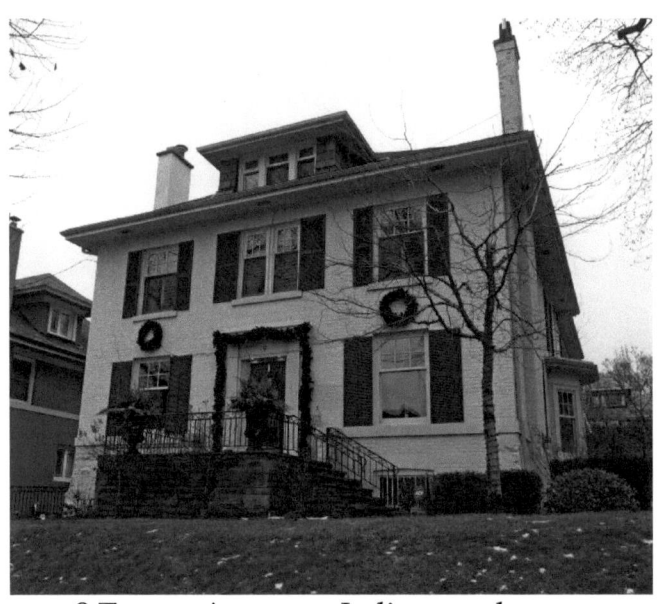

9 Turner Avenue – Italianate, dormer

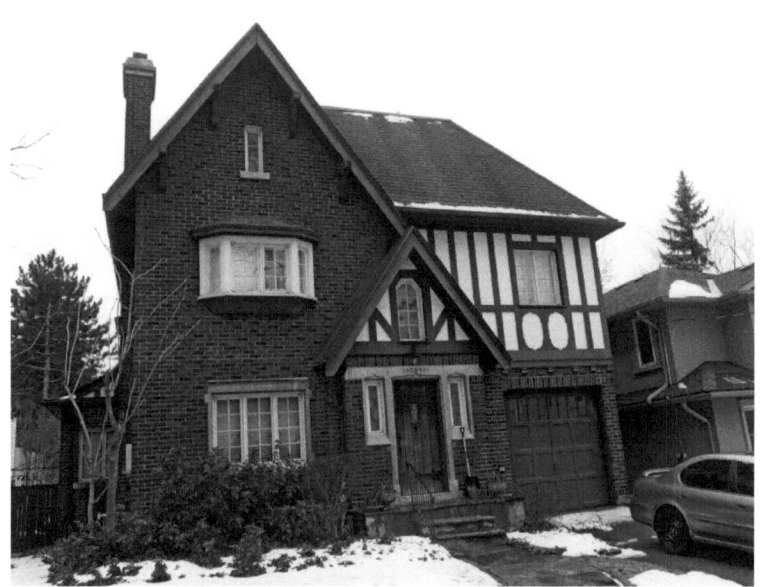

8 Turner Avenue – Tudor style

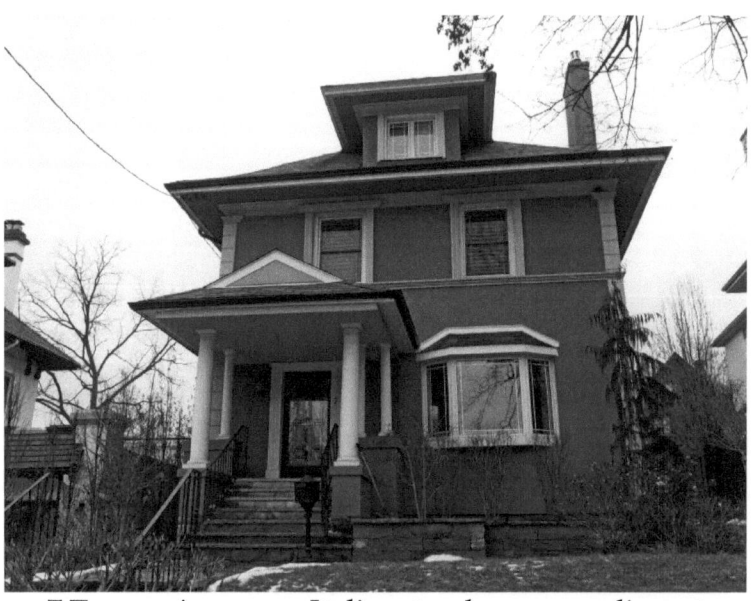

7 Turner Avenue – Italianate, dormer, pediment

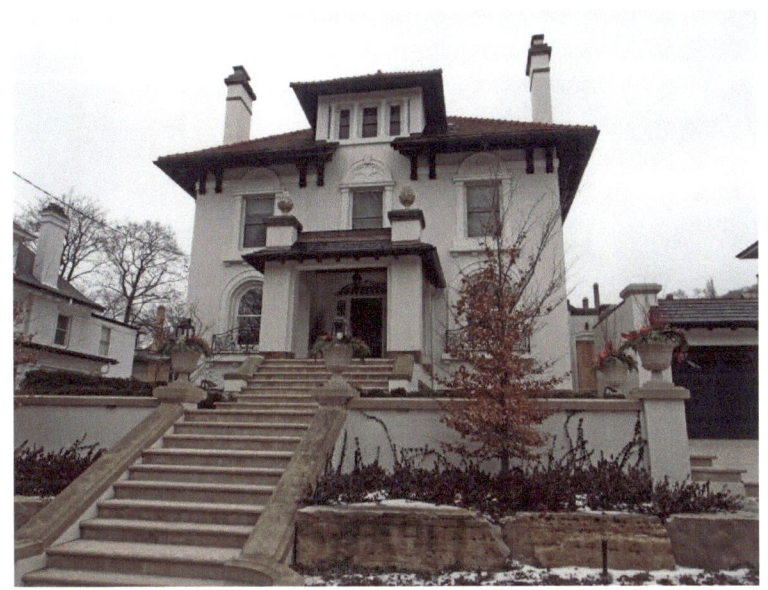

5 Turner Avenue – Italianate, dormer

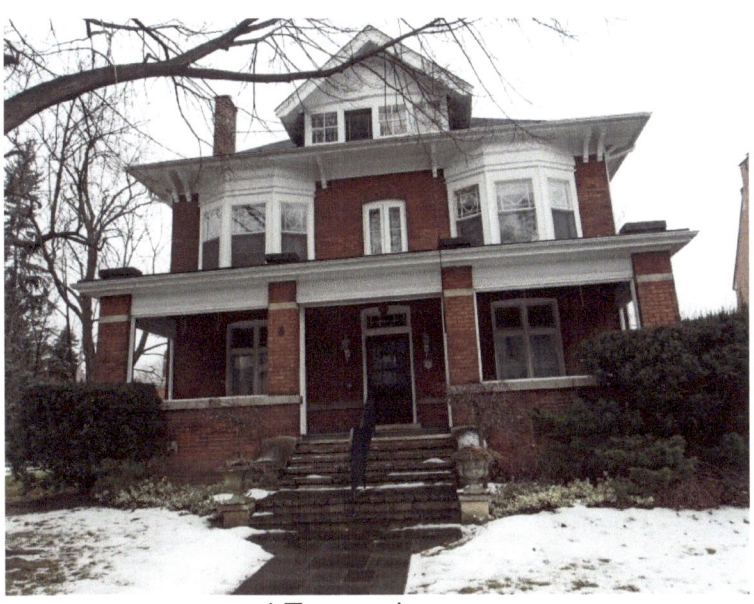

4 Turner Avenue

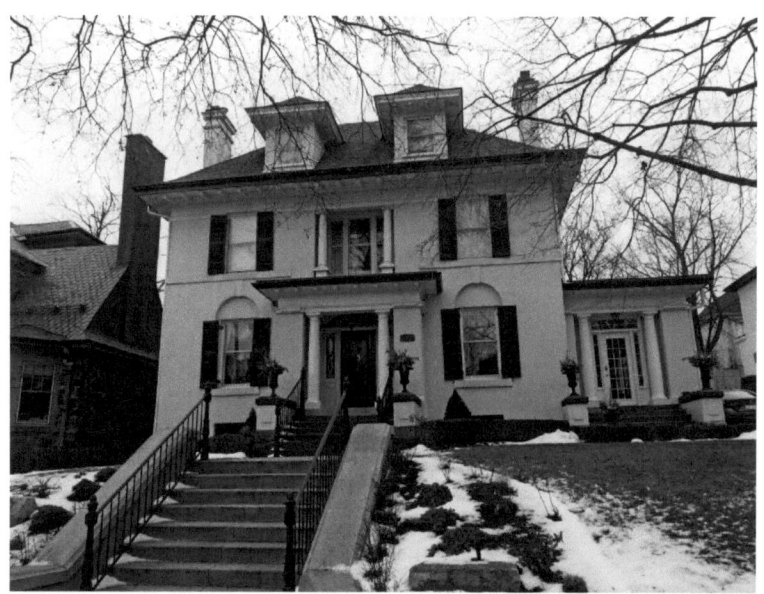

3 Turner Avenue – Italianate, dormers

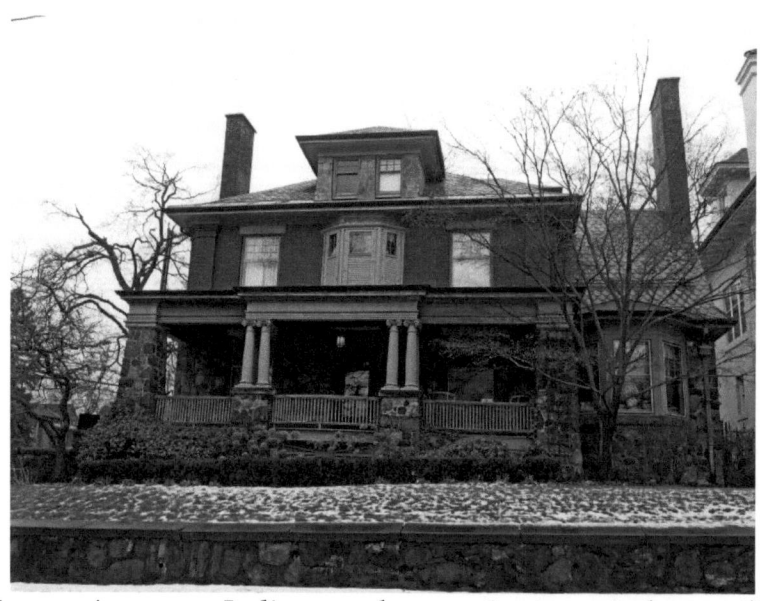

1 Turner Avenue – Italianate, dormer, Ionic capitals on pillars

Gloucester Road

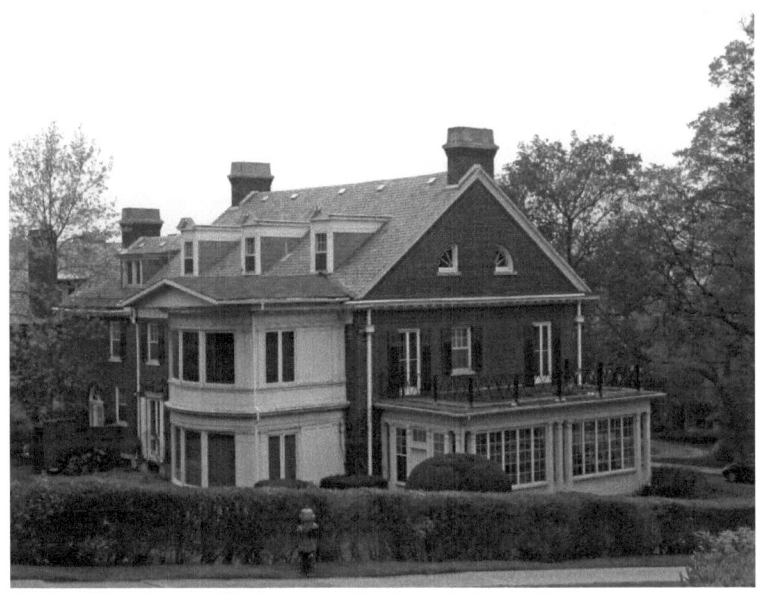

Dormers, balcony above enclosed sunroom

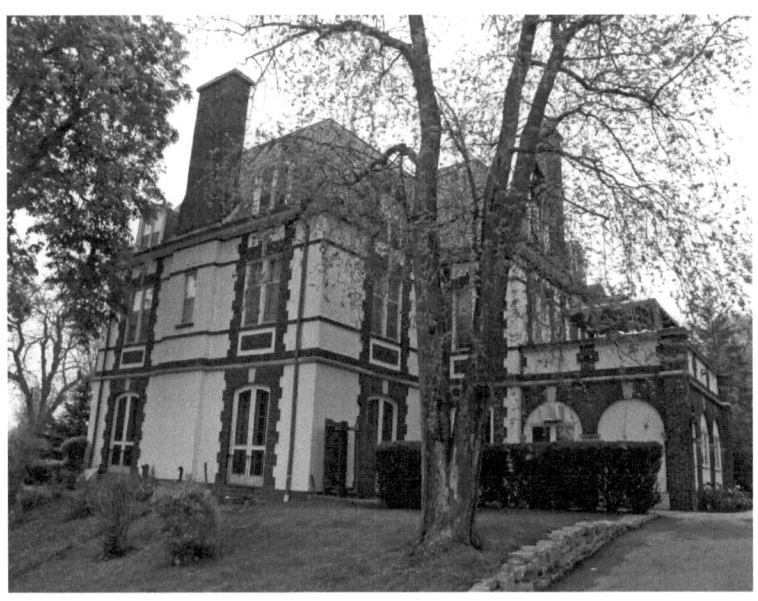

Architectural Terms

Banding: Different materials, colors or textures used in horizontal bands along a wall. Example: 39 Stanley Avenue, Page 28	
Battlement: A design for a parapet that has alternating solid parts and openings, originally used for defense, but later used as a decorative motif. Example: University Hall, Page 6	
Brackets: a decorative or weight-bearing structural element which forms a right angle with one side against a wall and the other under a projecting surface such as an eave or roof. Example: 97 Erie Avenue, Page 45	
Buttress: a masonry structure built against or projecting from a wall which serves to support or reinforce the wall. In Canadian architecture, they are sometimes used for decoration. Example: University Hall, Page 6	
Capital: The uppermost finish or decoration on a column. An Ionic column has a small base, a thin elegant shaft, and a capital composed of volutes which are carved whirls or twists that take the form of a scroll Example: 105 Erie Avenue, Page 46	
Cornice Return: decorative element on the end of a gable. Example: 39 Homewood Avenue, Page 34	
Dentil Moulding: an even series of rectangles used as ornamental decoration in cornices. Example: 105 Erie Avenue, Page 46	

Dichromatic brickwork: the use of two colours of brick, tile or slate to decorate a façade. Example: 30-32 Erie Avenue, Page 38	
Dormer: (French for "sleep") a gable end window that pierces through the plane of a sloping roof surface to create usable space in the top floor or attic of a building by adding headroom. Example: 55 Stanley Avenue, Page 29	
Fretwork: interlaced decorative design resembling a bracket Example: 105 Erie Avenue, Page 46	
Frontispiece: a portion of the façade of a building, usually a centred doorway that is slightly raised from the rest of the building, usually has extensive ornamentation. Frontispieces are usually Classical in design with white columned porches. Example: Westdale Secondary School, Page 22	
Gable: the triangular portion of a wall between the edges of a sloping roof. Example: 138 Erie Avenue, Page 47	
Hipped Roof: a roof where all sides slope downwards to the walls with no gables. Example: 83 Forsyth Avenue North, Page 17	

Keystones and Voussoirs: a voussoir is a wedge-shaped element used in building an arch. A keystone is the central stone that locks all the stones into position, allowing the arch to bear weight. A keystone is often enlarged and embellished. Example: 1 Stanley Avenue, Pg. 27	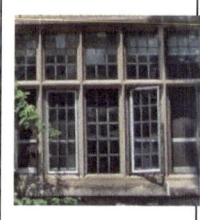
Mansard Roof: This style was popularized by Francois Mansart (1598-1666), an accomplished architect of the French Baroque period and especially fashionable during the Second French Empire (1852-1870). This roof is almost flat on the top section, with two slopes on each of its sides with the lower slope at a steeper angle than the upper and having dormer windows. Example: 30-32 Erie Avenue, Page 38	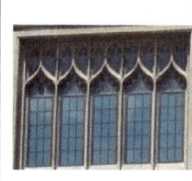
Muntin: When a window unit has more than one pane, the material that separates the panes is called the muntin. The larger, more decorative separations are called mullions. In stained glass windows, each piece of colored glass is held in place by a muntin. These were traditionally made of iron. Example: McMaster University Building, Page 9	
Ogee Arch: The ogee curve is created by the union of a concave and a convex arch. The result looks a bit like an S. This is used at the top of arches as well as for the profile of moldings. The ogee arch is Gothic in design. Example: Hamilton Hall, Page 7	

Oriel Window - These small areas were originally set into walls and galleries for the purpose of private prayer. Over time, any projecting window or area on an upper floor was called an oriel. Example: Hamilton Hall, Page 8	
Palladian Window: a large window that is divided into three sections with the centre section larger than the two side sections and usually arched. Example: 55 Stanley Avenue, Page 29	
Parapet: low wall around the edge of a roof. Parapet has battlementing. Example: University Hall, Page 6	
Pediment: a triangular section above the horizontal structure (entablature), typically supported by columns. The inside of the triangle is called the tympanum. Example: 105 Erie Avenue, Page 46	
Quoin: masonry blocks at the corner of a wall, often a decorative feature, usually larger or of a different colour than the rest of the wall. Example: 39 Homewood Avenue, Page 34	
Reveal: The vertical part of a jamb of an opening in a wall particularly a door or window that is visible between the door or window surface and outer wall surface. Reveals can be quite decorative or remarkable by their size. Example: Hamilton Hall, Page 8	

Spandrel: The area between the curve of an arch and the adjacent wall, or between two consecutive arches. Example: University Hall, Page 6	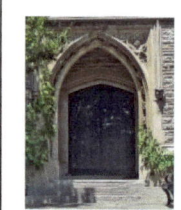
Tracery: A pattern of interlacing ribs carved or formed from stone and ornamenting a Gothic building, generally in the window and door areas as well as ceilings and staircases. The tracery is often foliated, or composed of different patterns of foils. Example: University Hall, Page 6	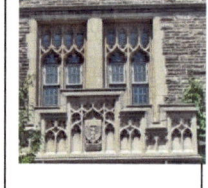
Turret: a small tower that projects from the wall of a building. Example: 20 Homewood Avenue, Page 36	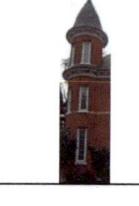
Verge board and Finial: also called bargeboards – hang from the projecting end of a roof and are often elaborately carved and ornamented. **Finial:** ornament added to the top of a gable, pinnacle, canopy or spire – a Gothic element. Example: 1 Stanley Avenue, Page 27	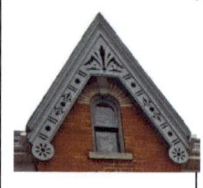
Window Hood: A **hood** is the piece found above window openings, usually of an ornate design, and covers the top third of the opening. Hoods are commonly placed above arched or curved openings on both windows and doors. Example: 30-32 Erie Avenue, Page 38	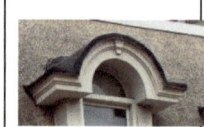

Building Styles

Edwardian, 1900-1930 – This style bridges the ornate and elaborate styles of the Victorian era and the simplified styles of the 20th century. Balanced facades, simple roof lines, dormer windows, large front porches, and smooth brick surfaces are its characteristics. Example: 58 Erie Avenue, Page 42	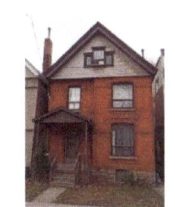
Classical Revival (1820 - 1860) – This style was an analytical, scientific, and dogmatic revival based on intensive studies of Greek and Roman buildings, concerned with the application of Greek plans and proportions to civic buildings. Schools, libraries, government offices, and most other civic buildings were built in the Classical Revival style. The white columned porches of the Classical Revival domestic buildings are identified with the mansions of wealthy land owners in Canada. Example: Hamilton Central Public School, Page 24	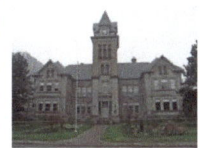
Gothic Revival, 1830-1890 – These decorative buildings have sharply-pitched gables with highly detailed verge boards, pointed-arch window openings, and dichromatic brickwork. It is a common style in Ontario. Example: Erie Avenue, Page 50	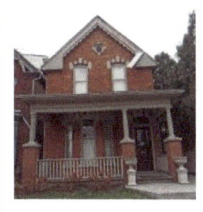

Italianate, 1850-1900 – It has wide-bracketed eaves, belvederes, wrap-around verandahs. Example: 48 Homewood Avenue, Page 32	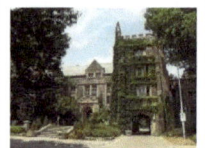
Neo-Gothic (Collegiate Gothic): is monochromatic and on a much grander scale than Gothic. Early Neo-Gothic was the decorative use of Gothic elements with a lack of knowledge and understanding of Gothic construction. Neo-Gothic tried to understand the basic principles of Gothic and used them. Materials used were natural stone combined with brick. Example: University Hall, Page 6	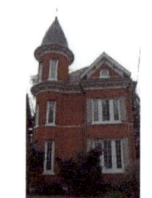
Queen Anne, 1885-1900 – This style is distinguished by an irregular outline featuring a combination of an offset tower, broad gables, projecting two-storey bays, verandahs, multi-sloped roofs, and tall, decorative chimneys. A mixture of brick and wood is common. Windows often have one large single-paned bottom sash and small panes in the upper sash. Example: 20 Homewood Avenue, Pg. 36	
Second Empire, 1860-1880 – The mansard roof is the most noteworthy feature of this style and is evidence of the French origins. Projecting central towers and one or two-storey bays can also be present. Example: 30-32 Erie Avenue, Page 38	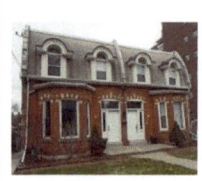

Victorian - In Ontario, a Victorian style building can be seen as any building built between 1840 and 1900 that doesn't fit into any of the other categories. It encompasses a large group of buildings constructed in brick, stone, and timber, using an eclectic mixture of Classical and Gothic motifs.

Example: Hunter Street West – Page 24 - remodeled in 1890 with a steeply pitched roof, round-arched windows and a higher central tower to conform to late Victorian tastes

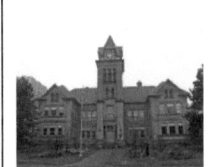

www.ingramcontent.com/pod-product-compliance
Lightning Source LLC
Chambersburg PA
CBHW040849180526
45159CB00001B/367